核心素养导向的
学科教学丛书

罗晓杰 张璐 洪艳◎编著

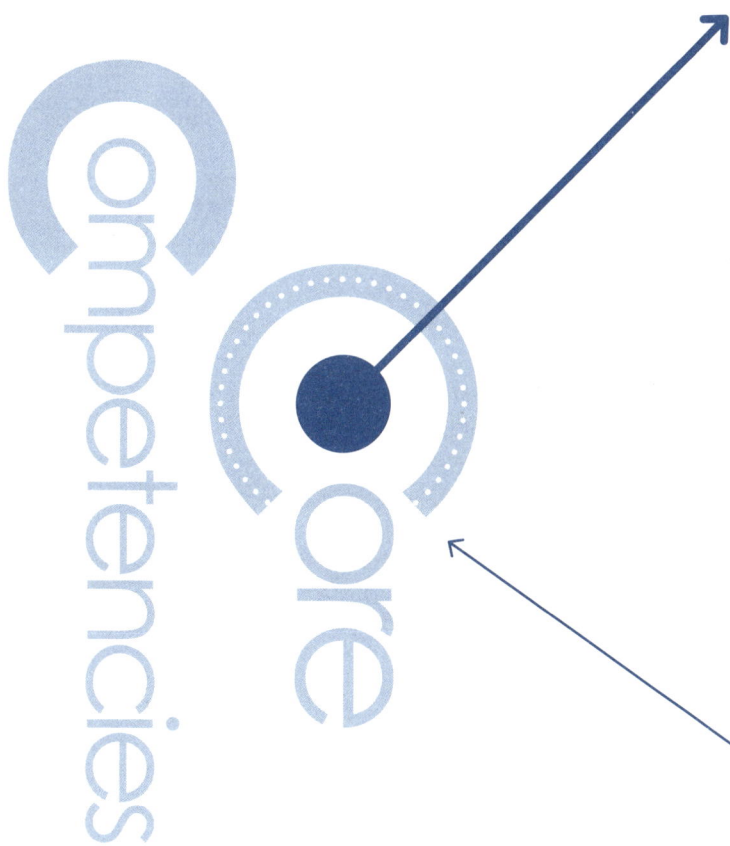

新设计，新说课

小学英语优质课例

Competencies

Core

华东师范大学出版社
上海

图书在版编目（CIP）数据

小学英语优质课例：新设计,新说课 / 罗晓杰,张璐,洪艳编著. —上海：华东师范大学出版社,2019
ISBN 978 - 7 - 5675 - 8682 - 6

Ⅰ.①小… Ⅱ.①罗… ②张… ③洪… Ⅲ.①英语课－教学研究－小学 Ⅳ.①G623.312

中国版本图书馆 CIP 数据核字(2019)第 044722 号

小学英语优质课例：新设计,新说课

编　　著	罗晓杰　张　璐　洪　艳
责任编辑	李恒平
特约审读	卢元珊
责任校对	时东明
装帧设计	卢晓红

出版发行　华东师范大学出版社
社　　址　上海市中山北路 3663 号　邮编 200062
网　　址　www.ecnupress.com.cn
电　　话　021 - 60821666　行政传真 021 - 62572105
客服电话　021 - 62865537　门市(邮购)电话　021 - 62869887
地　　址　上海市中山北路 3663 号华东师范大学校内先锋路口
网　　店　http://hdsdcbs.tmall.com/

印 刷 者　上海盛隆印务有限公司
开　　本　787 毫米×1092 毫米　1/16
印　　张　10.25
字　　数　223 千字
版　　次　2019 年 11 月第 1 版
印　　次　2023 年 12 月第 10 次
书　　号　ISBN 978 - 7 - 5675 - 8682 - 6
定　　价　42.00 元

出 版 人　王　焰

编委会

（按姓氏拼音排序）

前　言

　　本书主要面向在职小学英语教师、师范院校英语专业学生和学科教学（英语）专业研究生。本书按照评估型说课和教研型说课两类，分别呈现了对话课、语音课、阅读课、读写课、词汇课和复习课等小学英语常见课型的说课实录和教学设计，以帮助读者更好地把握说课内容、学习说课方法和提高说课艺术。

　　全书共分为三个组成部分。第一部分：英语学科说课概论。该部分简要介绍了英语学科说课的概念和类型，从说课功能角度将英语学科说课划分为评估型说课和教研型说课，从有无媒体辅助的角度将英语学科说课的类型划分为无辅助英语说课和多媒体辅助英语说课；系统介绍了说课的主要内容和方法，具体包括如何说教材、如何说学生、如何说重点和难点、如何说教材处理、如何说教学目标、如何说教学方法、如何说教学过程、如何说作业设计、如何说板书设计、如何说教学反思等具体的说课内容和方法。第二部分：小学英语评估型说课案例。该部分共呈现了十个小学英语常见课型的评估型说课案例（附教学设计），说课语言为英语。第三部分：小学英语教研型说课案例。该部分共呈现了两个教研型说课案例（附教学设计），说课语言为汉语。在教学设计中也给出了板书设计，以供读者更好地理解设计思路（为呈现真实情景中的板书，个别小问题未作处理）。

　　本书的突出特色是提供了优秀教师的说课视频。在第二部分和第三部分的每个说课案例后附说课视频的二维码，读者可以扫码观看说课视频，对照说课实录和说课视频体会说课的方法和艺术。多模态的说课示范为规范小学英语教师的说课行为和提高其说课水平提供了保障。

　　本书以英语说课理论为基础，以小学英语说课实践为落脚点，既有一定的理论高度，又有较高的实践操作价值，是作者长期从事英语学科说课理论研究与实践探索的智慧结晶。本书的说课案例均由作者与一线教师合作开发，理念先进的教学设计和精致的说课案例无疑将对一线小学英语教师、师范院校英语专业学生和学科教学(英语)专业研究生的教学设计与说课实践提供示范与指导。阅读本书对职前和在职小学英语教师的学科教学知识与能力的提高有很大裨益。

罗晓杰　浙江师范大学

2019 年 1 月 1 日

目　录

第一部分　英语学科说课概论

一、 英语学科说课的概念

英语说课是指按照说课常规要求,面向同行、教研人员等,使用英语(有时用汉语)分析教材和学生、陈述教学目标、描述教学过程和效果、说明作业和板书设计、总结教学亮点、反思教学问题及其原因的教研活动。

二、 英语学科说课的基本类型

从不同的角度可以将英语学科说课划分为不同的类型。按照说课的目的和用途,可将英语学科说课划分为评估型说课和教研型说课;按照说课过程有无媒体辅助,可将英语学科说课划分为无辅助英语说课和多媒体辅助英语说课。

(一) 评估型英语说课

评估型英语说课主要用于对英语教师的教学与教研能力的考查,通常用于在职教师或英语专业师范生的教师技能竞赛、英语教师入职考核、职称评定或教师招聘等。此类说课的语言通常为英语,通过说课评估说课者作为英语教师的专业技能和职业技能,反映说课者的英语学科教育教学能力和教育教学理论水平。

一般情况下,评估型说课有时间要求,对说课的准备时间也有要求,因此,也被称为限时说课,是较为科学的教师综合素质评价手段。对于英语学科评估型说课来说,使用英语说课更能正确反映说课者的英语教师素质,这是由英语学科的特殊性所决定的。

(二) 教研型英语说课

教研型英语说课可以进一步划分为集体备课用的教研型说课、课堂观摩前和课堂观摩后的教研型说课。集体备课用的教研型说课一般使用汉语,其操作程序为:指定 1—2 人先行说课,然后集体研讨,最后综合各方意见,形成最佳的教学设计方案。课堂观摩前后的教研型说课,其主要目的是为评课研讨活动提供上课和听课不能提供或无法获得的备课信息。课堂观摩前的教研型说课的主要操作程序是:说课—上课—评课研讨,参加研讨的教师可以根据教师上课和说课所提供的理论与实践两个方面的信息,把教师课前的"主观"设想(说课呈现)与课上"客观"的教学效果(上课呈现)进行比较、分析和研讨。课堂观摩后的教研型说课的主要操作程序是:上课—说课—评课研讨,参加研讨的教师可以根据教师的课堂教学实况和课后说课反思等相关信息展开专题研讨。

一般情况下,教研型英语说课没有严格的时间要求,被称为非限时说课,是更为规范和更高层次的教研活动。在教研型说课活动中,对英语学科使用英语还是使用汉语说课没有特殊要求,但由于参加教研活动的教师英语水平参差不齐,使用汉语说课更能保证教研效果。目前,我国英语教学界的教研活动通常采用课堂观摩后的教师说课。此类说课的目的在于教研,而不是评定英语教师的素质,故一般采用汉语说课。

(三)无辅助英语说课

由于英语学科的特殊性,有无媒体辅助说课,对说课教研的效果影响较大。因此,有必要细致区分无辅助说课与多媒体辅助说课。

无辅助说课是指按照说课常规要求,教师不借助任何辅助手段,面向同行、教研人员等,使用英语说明某单元或某节课的教学设计及其理论依据。使用英语进行无辅助说课,语言表达难度较大。由于教师使用英语分析教材和学情,陈述教学目标和重点难点,介绍教学方法和学习策略,描述教学活动及设计意图,那些不常用的教学术语无疑会增加听者对说课内容的理解难度,如果说者不降低英语难度,不使用肢体语言辅助说课,不能根据现场反馈调整语速以便与听者的思维保持同步,那么,说课的效果会大打折扣。

(四)多媒体辅助英语说课

使用英语进行多媒体辅助说课可以降低英语学科的说课难度。与无辅助英语说课相比较,使用英语进行多媒体辅助说课在说课内容上没有发生大的方向性的变化。由于使用多媒体技术,声音、图像、文本信息与"说"的内容可以同步呈现,能增强"说"课内容的直观性,有助于听者想象和推测课堂教学情境。因为幻灯片放映不但能引导听者思路,还能丰富听者对教学情境的想象,帮助听者推测课堂教学效果。CAI(Computer-Assisted Instruction 计算机辅助教学)课件呈现的教学信息,作为教师"说"的有效补充和延伸,弥补了无辅助英语说课不易直接理解的不足。值得注意的是,使用英语进行多媒体辅助说课也有一定的难度,如果幻灯片播放和说课的语言配合不好,文本信息的选择与呈现的量、度把握不准,则会影响说课效果。使用汉语进行多媒体辅助说课,则难度不大。如果使用汉语进行教研型课后说课,借助多媒体展示教学课例,说课效果会大大提高。

三、 英语学科说课的内容模块

英语学科说课的内容包括说教材、说学生、说重点和难点、说教材处理、说教学目标、说教学方法、说学习方法、说教学媒体、说设计思路、说教学过程、说教学效果、说作业设计、说板书设计、说教学亮点、说教学不足等。各说课要点之间内容交叉且关系紧密,绝对区分的线性说课将导致说课内容重复。鉴于大多数说课限定时间,为了避免重复,本书将评估型英语说课的内容划分为五个模块,将教研型英语说课的内容划分为三个模块。各模块内容要素相对稳定,模块内部内容可以相互融合,以便灵活应对说课时间和内容要求。

对于评估型说课而言，"分析""陈述""描述"和"说明"四个模块更加重要。因为上述模块内容能够反映说课者的教学设计能力以及教育教学理论水平。对于教研型说课而言，反思目标达成过程中的教学得失更为重要。因为听者就在上课现场观摩教学，教学目标、目标达成度以及对教学效果的反思更能体现和发挥说课在教学研讨中的作用。

（一）评估型英语说课的内容模块

评估型英语说课的内容可划分为"分析""陈述""描述""说明"和"反思"五个模块。具体模块及内容要素如下：

模块一　"分析"教材和学生。该模块主要包括说教材和说学生。说教材主要分析教材内容，分析教材的地位和作用；说学生主要分析学生的知识与技能基础、分析学生的学习兴趣和认知风格。分析教材和学生有助于确定重点和难点。

模块二　"陈述"目标和方法。该模块具体包括说教学目标和说教学方法。教学目标主要基于教材和学生分析确定，教师在明确重点和难点后，基于学情处理教材和选择教学方法。

模块三　"描述"过程和效果。该模块主要包括说教学过程（有时只说教学思路）和说教学效果。说教学过程主要按照时间顺序说明本节课的教学活动顺序，描述师生互动过程；说教学效果可以从教学设计的出发点的角度说设计意图，或者从教学实施的落脚点的角度说预设的效果。"描述"过程和效果既要形象生动，又要有理有据，以便帮助听者想象教学过程的实施和理解教学活动的设计。

模块四　"说明"作业与板书。该模块主要包括说作业设计和说板书设计，说明作业设计和板书设计的意图及其对学生英语学习的促进作用。

模块五　"反思"亮点与不足。该模块主要包括说教学亮点和设计不足，说明该教学设计体现的先进教学理念和有效教学活动。

在评估型英语说课中，我们没有把教学的重点和难点归到任何一个模块，这并非因为它们不是说课的重点。恰恰相反，正是因为它们非常重要，每一个模块都需要关注教学的重点和难点，并需要将其融合到五个模块之中，贯穿说课的全程。说课教师应结合教材和学生进行分析，说明重点和难点确定的依据；结合教学目标陈述，明确重点和难点；结合教学过程描述、作业设计和板书设计，说明突出重点和突破难点的活动设计和实施方法；结合教学反思说明如何进一步突出重点和突破难点，达成教学目标。总之，说重点难点是不可或缺的重要说课内容，需要多次与五个模块的说课内容融合。

（二）教研型英语说课的内容模块

教研型英语说课的内容可划分为"教学目标定位""教学目标达成度"和"教学得失反思"三个模块。具体模块及内容要素如下：

模块一　"教学目标定位"。该模块主要包括说教材、说学生、说重点难点和说教学目标。通过分析教材内容和学生的知识技能基础，说明教学的重点和难点是什么，从而确立本堂课的教学目标。

模块二 "教学目标达成度"。该模块主要包括说教材处理、说教法学法、说教学设计思路、说教学过程和说作业设计。具体围绕教学过程,说明为了突出重点、突破难点和达成教学目标,教师对教材进行了怎样的处理,选择和使用何种教法或学法,如何利用教学媒体,按照怎样的教学思路实施教学活动和布置作业。

模块三 "教学得失反思"。该模块主要包括说教学效果、说教学亮点、说教学不足和说再教设计。具体反思教学设计所体现的先进教学理念,反思在教学实施过程中师生互动是否有效,教学目标为何有效达成或效果欠佳,再教本课会进行怎样的改进。

四、 英语学科说课的内容与方法

(一)说教材

说教材应简要介绍教材内容的各个组成部分以及各部分之间的逻辑关系;正确解读教材文本及其编写意图;分析教材的主要内容及其难易度和学生必备的知识和技能,分析本课教学内容对本章节学习的影响与意义,说明教材的地位和作用,为重点和难点的确定提供支撑。

(二)说学生

说学生应分析并明确学生原有的知识基础和技能水平与本课应达到的知识与技能水平之间的差距;说明学生对所学内容的熟悉和熟练程度;分析学生的学习能力、认知风格、学习兴趣和情感态度等。换句话说,教师应说清学生与本课内容直接相关的知识技能欠缺,以及与本课教学内容和方法直接相关的智力和非智力影响因素,为难点的确定提供支撑。

(三)说重点和难点

说重点和难点应说明本节课的重点和难点是什么;重点的选择是否符合英语学科课程标准要求和教材编写意图;难点的确定是否符合教材和学生实际。

(四)说教材处理

说教材处理主要说清对教材内容做了怎样的取舍,改编或增加了什么内容和活动,对哪些内容和活动的顺序进行了调整,删除或替换了哪些内容或活动。说教材处理要考虑到新旧知识的联结,要考虑教材处理是否有利于知识的迁移,处理后的教材是降低了难度还是提高了难度,在多大程度上促进重点的突出、难点的突破和教学目标的达成。

(五)说教学目标

说教学目标主要基于教材和学生分析,主要说明通过本节课教学,学生学得的语言知识、文化知识和掌握的语言技能,以及在学习过程中思维品质、学习能力和文化意识的提升。

英语学科核心素养的四维目标是相对可分、相互融合的。因此,说教学目标也没有必要按照四个维度逐条陈述,无论逐条或是融合说教学目标,只要能够涵盖本节课的目标要素,都是可以的,因为上述目标均有意义上的交叉,并以共同的教学内容为载体,共同服务于培养学生综合语言运用能力的总体目标。

说教学目标可以结合教学过程、教学反思或教学亮点来进行。结合教学过程,可以说某一教学活动的效果如何,达成了什么目标;结合教学反思,可以说本节课教学效果如何,哪些目标达成度高,哪些目标还需要下节课进一步落实。

(六) 说教学方法

说教学方法应说清本节课教师采用的教学方法或教学模式,解读所选教学方法或教学模式的核心理念、操作方法和主要特色。说教学方法要清楚地说明在教学过程中教师如何使用该方法开展教学活动,引导、组织学生参与,启发学生理解知识和训练技能。说教学方法时可结合教学媒体选择和教学过程设计说明如何有效使用该教学方法或教学模式。说教学方法还要说清该教学方法选择是否符合教学实际和学生实际,对教师传授知识和学生发展能力有何助益。说教学方法通常还要说明教师使用何种教学媒体辅助教学,媒体辅助教学的效果也可以结合教学过程说明。

说教学方法还可以从学生学的角度说明本节课学习过程中,学生使用或学习使用了什么学习方法,效果如何,说清学生在可能出现的学习困境中,教师如何指导学生运用恰当的学习方法或策略理解知识和训练技能,指导学生掌握并有效利用该学习方法发现问题、分析问题和解决问题,说明学法指导是否有助于发展学生的学习技能或培养学生的学习能力等。

(七) 说教学过程

说教学过程要说明本节课包括哪几个教学环节,各教学环节的名称和所需的教学时间。一般情况下,说教学过程要按照时间顺序说明每个教学环节包括哪些教学活动,每个教学活动中师生互动如何开展,该教学活动的设计意图是什么或可能的教学效果如何。说教学过程重在说明教学活动过程中教师如何组织活动,怎样启发诱导,为学生指点迷津,怎样指导学生自主探究,为学生排疑解难,如何突出重点和突破难点,等等。

在进行教研型说课时,说教学过程比较简单,主要说明教学的总体设计思路,说明教学过程推进的过程中,各教学环节的逻辑关系,以帮助听者从整体上把握教学过程展开的逻辑顺序。教研型说课时,说教学过程一般与说教学目标达成情况相结合,即在教学过程中,学生的语言能力、学习能力、思维品质和文化意识得到了怎样的发展,在课堂上是否学会相关的语言知识和文化知识,是否熟练掌握了相关的语言技能,获得了怎样的情感体验和文化理解,等等。

(八) 说作业设计

说作业设计要说清作业的内容、类型和要求,完成作业的方式、作业的检测或评价方法和该作业设计意图等。说作业设计重在说明作业设计意图。说作业设计意图要说明该作业是旨在加深对知识的理解,还是运用所学知识技能;是巩固所学的知识,还是拓宽视野、提升能力。

(九) 说板书设计

说板书设计要说清板书的主要内容、整体布局及其展开程序,说明板书的功能、效果和设计意图。

不同类型的说课对说板书设计的要求也不尽相同。进行评估型英语说课时,教师可以边说课边板书,板书内容随着说课内容的推进而有序呈现,在说课结束前,板书的主要内容应该基本呈现在黑板上。因此,评估型说课时真正说板书设计用时不多,板书内容与布局只要简单概括即可,重在说明板书设计意图。进行教研型说课时,由于听者在上课和说课的现场,能够直接感受板书的展开顺序,板书已经在上课后完整地呈现出来了,因此,说板书设计也只需说明板书设计意图及其对学生学习的作用。

(十) 说教学反思

说教学反思要说明本节课的成功之处、不足之处或值得商榷的问题。说教学成功之处要具体说明教学的精心设计或师生出色的课堂表现;说不足之处要反思教学疏漏之处或效果不佳的根本原因。教研型说课一般还要说值得商榷的问题,针对教学设计与实际教学的疏漏进行再教设计。

第二部分　小学英语评估型说课案例

说课案例一（对话课）

PEP 5　Unit 5　There is a big bed　B Let's talk

微课

Hello，everyone. I'm happy to present my lesson plan here. I'm Zheng Zhenzhen from Wenzhou Shuangchao Primary School. Today I will present my lesson from 5 aspects.

I. Analysis

The teaching material is from PEP Book 5. Unit 5 *There is a big bed*. The theme of this unit is "rooms and household articles" with the function of describing positions. It's the continuation of room series. In PEP Book 3，Unit 4 *My home*，students have already learned about rooms and furniture. And students will continue to learn the question-form of *There be* structure in Unit 6 *In a nature park*. So Unit 5 is also the preparation for Unit 6. This unit includes 6 periods. In the 1st and 2nd periods，students have already learned about the singular form of *There be* structure. This lesson is the 3rd period. The lesson type is listening and speaking. Students will learn to describe things and their positions with the plural form of *There be* structure.

My students are in Grade 5. Generally speaking，they are active，curious and interested in learning new things. And after learning English for more than 2 years，most of them have formed good English learning habits. Besides，they are familiar with the theme，and they have already obtained certain previous knowledge about it. Therefore，the learning difficulties will be greatly reduced. So I will provide some key sentence structures for students to express themselves more fluently and freely.

II. Statement

Based on the analysis of the teaching material and the learners，the following learning objectives are to be achieved in this lesson：

1) Communicative competence：Firstly，with the help of teacher，students will be able to understand the meaning of the dialogue，useful words and expressions like

grandparents, *their*, *house*, *flowers*, *lots of*, and they will be able to use them skillfully in a real communicative context. Secondly, students can proficiently use *There be* structure to describe things and their positions in a place. They can read the dialogue aloud with correct pronunciation, intonation and stress, and act it out.

2) Cognitive and thinking ability: Firstly, students will be able to improve their evaluating and applying abilities by the evaluation and discussion of Zhang Peng's living room and the description of their own living rooms. Secondly, students will be able to promote their analyzing ability by mind map and the reconstruction of the text.

3) Social-cultural awareness: Firstly, students will be willing to describe things and their positions in English. Secondly, students' love to family members will be evoked as well.

III. Description

OK, here comes the teaching procedure. There are 3 stages in my lesson. Look at the whole design (pointing at PPT). I will make full use of pictures talking about Zhang Peng's photo, pictures in the living room, about pictures drawn by his father, and about the photo of grandparents' garden and photos of students' home. They are combined to form the topic chain of this lesson. Now let me work stage by stage.

In the revision and lead-in stage, students will firstly sing a song together to liven up the classroom atmosphere. And then they will be asked to look at the picture of Zhang Peng's bedroom and guess the things in it. This activity is mainly designed to activate students' background knowledge and lead in the next stage more naturally and vividly. It also helps cultivate students' confidence of speaking English. In the second stage, there are four steps with several activities in each. These four steps are closely related to today's topic: talking about pictures.

Step 1 is about learning *Let's try* on P51. Firstly, students will be asked to guess the things in Zhang Peng's living room. Then they will listen to the recording carefully and tick the right answer on P51. Guessing before listening enables students to better understand the general idea of the listening material. Secondly, students will try to understand the meaning of "There are some nice pictures here." through a close study of this picture. Besides, they will try to find out the grammatical rule of *There are* structure in comparison with *There is* structure by themselves. Students can have a better understanding of There be structure during the grammar induction process in which the students will think, analyze and summarize the grammatical rule. They will know not only its meaning but also its formation and function. Their thinking qualities will be trained as well. Thirdly, students will be asked to work in pairs to talk about their own bedrooms with *There is* and *There are* structures. This activity is designed to practice *There be* structure in time, which reflects the migration of in-classroom learning to real-life situation. It also helps to deal with the language focus of this class: to use *There are* structure in a real communicative context. Fourthly, I'll ask the students to imitate the whole dialogue and pay special attention to the pronunciation, intonation and stress. This activity is designed to get students ready for the next step.

Step 2 is about learning *Let's talk* on p51. At the end of *Let's try*, Zhang Peng invites the children to visit his living room. So, at the very beginning, students will be asked to listen to the first part of the recording "This is the living room. There are so many pictures here". And I will ask students two questions "Where are the children?" and "What are they talking about now?" And then I will draw students' attention to the pictures on the wall and ask another question "Where are the pictures from?" Students will think, guess and talk freely. Pictures here are fully used to arouse students' curiosity so that they will be involved into learning all the time. Their interest in speaking in English will be aroused as well. Secondly, students will be asked to listen to the whole recording once and answer two questions. According to these two questions, I will divide the learning of *Let's talk* into two parts: A. Talking about Father's pictures; B. Talking about the photo of grandparents' garden. In the first part, students will be asked to practice the target language "I can ... Can you ... well?" in pairs. This activity is designed to let students use language to communicate with others. Then I will draw students' attention to this picture and ask, "Is this picture drawn by Father, too?" The students will guess and talk freely. So, the picture on p52 will be introduced at this time. Well, this picture provides a perfect context for learning. Through a close study of this picture, students will learn the meaning and usage of "in front of, their house, lots of flowers and so many" more freely and comfortably. Thirdly, students will listen to the dialogue and mark the intonation. Then they will listen and imitate, read aloud and act the dialogue out. Through Activity 3, students' pronunciation, intonation and liaison will be improved.

In Step 3, students will give an oral report on the topic of "pictures" with the help of the "picture mind map" on the screen and expressions on the blackboard. This activity will greatly improve students' ability of reorganizing and summarizing.

In Step 4, students will pay attention to the family photos on the wall. They will think, discuss and talk with their partners about the reasons why there are family photos on the wall. This topic is close to students' daily life, and they can learn something from their partners. So it is not difficult for them to draw the conclusion that Zhang Peng's family is full of love. They love each other, and they express love through family photos. So, the emotional objective works by itself.

Now it comes to the last stage: Consolidation and production. Firstly, students will watch a video prepared by themselves before class. In this video, some of them will introduce their homes, which are comfortable and full of love. The purpose is to elicit students' emotion and sentiments towards love and warmth so as to lay the foundation for the next activity — talking about your beautiful home. Next, students will be asked to work in groups to discuss, talk and make a new dialogue. The purpose of making a new dialogue is to check if students can use the key words and *There-be* structure correctly and skillfully. Students' ability of communication and cooperation will be developed as well during the learning process.

IV. Exposition

Here is my blackboard design. It is designed according to the lesson processing (Talking about Zhang Peng's bedroom→Pictures drawn by Father→Photo of grandparents' garden) with key words and important structures below. The above blackboard design helps students clarify their thinking and consolidate what they have learned.

Here is the homework design. Firstly, listen to the recording and read the dialogue on P51. Secondly, talk about their photos with their friends and give presentation next time. Homework 1 will help students to consolidate what they have learned. Homework 2 is designed to encourage students to use language to communicate with their friends.

V. Reflection

To sum up, the design of my lesson has some shining points. Firstly, preparing the lesson with an overall perspective. I find that pictures can be seen here and there in this unit. So I regard "pictures" as an important clue. I integrate the pictures of *A Talk* and *B Learn* into the learning process. All the activities are designed to talk about pictures. Such kind of reorganization makes teaching and learning more effective. Secondly, in this lesson, students develop their autonomous learning and cooperative learning strategies through various kinds of activities. For example, while learning the plural form of *There be* structure, students are encouraged to perform autonomous learning. By comparing "There is …" with "There are …", students will find out the similarities and differences between the two. This will greatly develop students' ability to observe, compare and summarize.

So much for my presentation. Thanks a lot for your attention.

(说课稿撰写者：温州市双潮小学　郑珍珍)

一、教学背景

1. 教材分析

本课是对话课,内容选自人教版《英语》五年级上册第5单元 *There is a big bed* 中的B部分,单元主题是"房间及家具"。由于学生在四年级上册第4单元 *My home* 中已经学习了各个房间和部分家具的英语表达,因此本单元在主题和知识点方面起着承接四上第四单元的作用;同时,学生将会在五年级下册第6单元 *In a nature park* 中继续学习 There be 句型的疑问句形式,因此本单元在知识点上起着"启下"的作用。本单元包含6个课时,学生在第一、二课时,已经学习了 There be 句型的单数形式。本课是第3课时,课型为听说课,继续探讨如何使用 There be 句型的复数形式去描述某处的物品构成。

2. 学情分析

本课学习对象是小学五年级学生,他们生性活泼好动,具有较强的好奇心和表现欲。经过两年多的英语学习,他们已经掌握了一定的学习方法,形成了比较良好的语言习惯。"房间与家具"主题与学生密切相关,学生有话可说、有话想说;并且通过之前的学习,学生在房间、家具、文具和形容词方面亦有所积累,这极大地降低了本课时的学习难度,因此教师着重在主题背景下提炼支架语言,帮助学生进行语言和情感的表达。

二、教学目标

1. 语言交际目标

(1)能够在图片和教师的帮助下理解对话大意以及 grandparents,their,house,flower,lots of 的意思并能够在语境中正确运用。

(2)能够在一定的语言情境中熟练运用 There be 句型来描述某处存在某事物,并能按照正确的语音、语调及意群朗读对话以及进行角色扮演。

2. 思维认知目标

(1)能够通过对张鹏照片的评价,讨论张鹏家客厅及描述自己家的客厅,实现语言的迁移和实际运用,提高评价与应用的认知能力。

(2)能够通过思维导图,提炼并重构文本,提升分析层面上的认知能力。

3. 社会文化目标

(1)能够乐于用英语描述家里的物品。

(2)能够体会有爱才有家,让爱天天住我家的爱家、爱家人、爱他人的情感。

三、 教学重难点

1. 教学重点：

对 There be 句型复数形式的理解和在情境中正确描述物品位置。

2. 教学难点：

对 There be 句型复数形式中 be 动词与后面名词复数的正确对应使用。

四、 教学准备

PPT；单词卡片；可粘贴的 3 张场景图片（bedroom， living room， grandparents' garden）；学生课前准备的自己家的照片。

五、 教学过程

Stage 1 Revision and lead-in(5 mins)

Activity 1：Sing a song

Sing the song "A photo of me" together.

Lyrics

A photo of me

Beside the big plant，what can you see?

Above the big clock，there's a photo of me.

Beside the big plant，what can you see?

Between the two windows，there's a photo of me.

Activity 2：Look and say

Talk about the picture of Zhang Peng's photo with "There is a/an ... in/on ...".

T：Look，this is Zhang Peng's bedroom. What's in the bedroom?

S1：...

（Then students are asked to pay attention to Zhang Peng's photo on the wall.）

T：What do you think of him in this photo?

S1：(I think he is cool/pretty/wonderful ...)

T：Oh, you think he is cool/pretty/wonderful ... Others?

S2：I ...

T：OK, you have different opinions. And what do Sarah and Mike think? Now let's listen to the recording.

> **Listening script**
>
> Mike：This picture is pretty.
>
> Sarah：Yes. I like it，too.
>
> Zhang Peng：Let's go to the living room.
>
> Mike & Sarah：OK！

【设计说明】 激活学生已有的知识储备,复习 There be 句型单数形式的用法。随后师生聚焦本课第一个微话题—Zhang Peng's photo,评价张鹏的照片,培养学生总结和评价的能力;泛听 B Let's try,获知 Mike 和 Sarah 对照片的评价,并且得知他们相约参观客厅,在情境上为 B Let's try 的学习进行铺垫。

Stage 2　Presentation and practice (20 mins)

Step 1 Let's try (p51)

Activity 1：Listen and tick

First talk about things in the living room freely，then listen to the recording and check it out.

T：Now we know the children are going to the living room. What's in Zhang Peng's living room? Can you guess?

S：...

T：OK. Now let's listen to the recording and try to tick the right answer：What's in the living room?

☐ Some pictures　　☐ Some flowers　　☐ Some toys

【设计说明】 通过听前预测活动集中学生注意力,提高听力效果。

Activity 2：Let's learn

Guess the meaning of "There are some nice pictures there." and find out the rules of "There are … " by themselves.

T：Look，Zhang Peng says that there are some nice pictures. So what does he mean? You may search this picture for some clues.

S1：(意思是"很棒的照片"。)

T：Wonderful！We can say，"There **is a** nice picture." And we also can say，" There **are** some nice picture**s** ".

What's the point here?

S2：(is 后面接单数名词, are 后面接复数名词。)

S3：(它们的意思都是说"有什么东西"。)

【设计说明】 学生初步感知本课语言重点。教师不是直接告知本课语言重点,而是由学生自己结合图片去感知和总结,能够培养学生的思维认知能力。

Activity 3：Let's say

A. Describe Zhang Peng's living room.

T：There are some nice pictures in the living room. There is a big fishbowl, too. What else can you see?

S1：There is a nice TV.

S2：There are some green plants.

S3：...

B. Describe your own living room.

T：There are so many things in Zhang Peng's living room. Now I want to know your living rooms. What's in your living room?

S1：There is ... in my living room.

S2：There are ... in my living room.

【设计说明】 语言的学习应是循环渐进的,操练环节滚动复习 There be 句型的单、复数形式;讨论张鹏家客厅后,学生接着说一说自己家的客厅,实现语言的迁移和实际运用。

Activity 4：Let's read

Read after the tape recording and imitate the pronunciation, intonation and stress.

【设计说明】 师生跟着录音一起朗读 Let's try 部分的文本,巩固所学知识"There *are* ... *n*s.",知识点的承接上为 Talk 的学习打下牢固基础,在情境上自然导入 B Let's talk 部分的学习。

Step 2 Let's talk (p51)

Activity 1：Listen and guess

Listen to the first part of *Let's talk* and answer the questions.

T：The children are talking in the living room now. What are they talking about? Let's listen.

Listening script

This is the living room. There are so many pictures here.

S1：Pictures.

T：Right! They are talking about the pictures in the living room. Would you try to guess where the pictures are from?

S1：（可能是他们买的图片。）

S2：（可能是别人送给他们的。）

S3：（可能是张鹏画的。）

S4：（可能是爸爸画的。）

S5：...

【设计说明】 教师在 pictures 上面巧做文章，挖掘图片潜在信息，合理猜测图片来历，使学生"身临其境"，引发学生的学习兴趣。

Let's think

Where are they from?
What do you think of them?

Activity 2：Listen and answer

Answer two questions according to the recording：

① Who can draw very well in Zhang Peng's family?

② Whose plants are those?

【设计说明】 教师根据下一步教学任务的需求将文本学习划分为 Father's pictures 和 Grandmother's plants 两部分，并提炼出两个提纲式的问题，并为下一步的教学做好准备。

A. Talk about Father's pictures

　　Practice saying：Can you ... very well? — Yes. /No.

T：Zhang Peng says ... （Teacher plays the recording：My father can draw very well. ）So his father can draw and he is good at drawing. I can speak English. What can you do?

S1：I can draw/...

T：Can you draw/... very well?

S1：Yes，I can. I can ... very well. /No，I can't. I can't ... very well.

T：OK. What can Wang Jia do? And Li Wei? Now please work in pairs to ask your partners.

【设计说明】 教师根据文本内容引导学生进行知识迁移，运用目标语言谈论自己的情况。

B. Talk about grandparents' plants

Learn the new words and phrases：*their house*，*in front of*，*lots of* and *grandparents'*.

What's this?
Whose garden?

T：What about this picture? Is it drawn by Father，too?

S：Yes. /No.

T：Look， Zhang Peng says， "My grandparents have a garden in front of their house. " What does "in front of" mean? （Teacher sticks "in front of" on the blackboard. ）

15

T：What's in the garden?

S1：(There are plants.)

T：Right! There are so many plants here.
（Teacher sticks "so many" on the blackboard.）

S2：(There are flowers.)

T：So there are lots of flowers in it.
（Teacher sticks "lots of" on the blackboard.）

My grandparents have a garden in front of their house.

A. 在前面   B. 在后面

【设计说明】 教师统整本单元资源,引入 B Learn 的内容,学生在一个有机的、有意义的、有联系的语境中学习并运用本课时所学的新词,同时教学也始终扣紧本课话题 pictures,由图入手,以图导听导说,在图片所描述的情境中结束学习任务。

Activity 3：Read and act

A. Listen to the dialogue and mark the tone, stress and liaisons.

B. Read after the recording and practice reading.

C. Act out the dialogue in groups of four.

【设计说明】 学生小组之间朗读、操练并分角色表演对话。该活动的设计既可以检测学生对文本的理解与掌握,又关注到学生的语音、语调状况。

Step 3　Try to say

Give an oral report on the topic of "pictures" with the help of the "picture mind map" on the screen and phrases on the blackboard.

Try to say　结合图片,尝试将课堂上所谈论的话题串联起来。
下面的句子结构可以帮助大家哟!

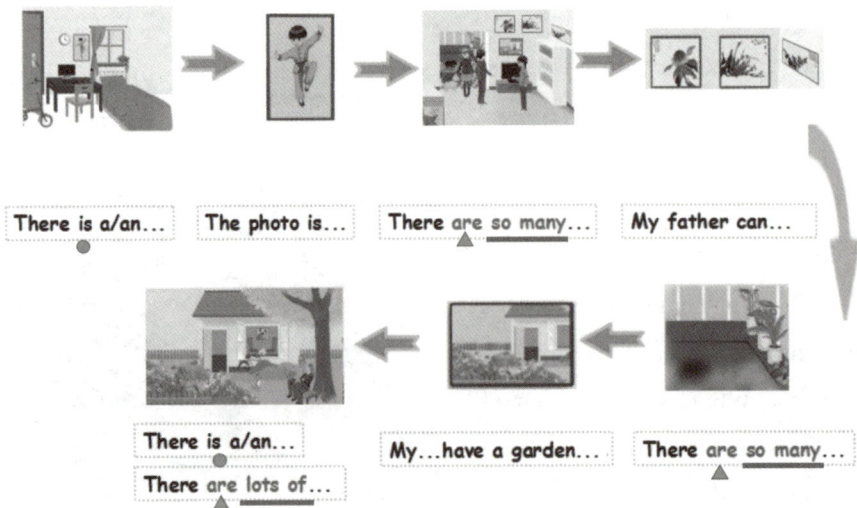

There is a/an...　The photo is...　There are so many...　My father can...

There is a/an...
There are lots of...

My...have a garden...　There are so many...

Step 4　Let's discuss

Discuss and understand the love among family members.

What's in your home?

T：You see，these pictures are called "family photos". In Chinese we call them "Quan jia fu". So where can we see a family photo?

S1：In our home，on the wall.

S2：On the desk.

S3：In our phone.

S4：In our computer.

S5：...

T：Quite true! You see they hang each other's family photos on the wall. So why? Please discuss with your partner.

S1：Because they love each other.

S2：They can see each other.

S3：They miss each other.

T：Right! We usually treasure others' photos because of love. Do you have family photos? Are they on the wall，too? Now take out your pictures，please.

Stage 3　Consolidation and production (9 mins)

Activity 1：Let's enjoy

With a piece of beautiful music，students enjoy a short video shot by some students in advance.

> **Narrator**
>
> Hello，this is my living room. It is pretty. There is a big TV. There are two sofas. There is a family photo on the wall. They are my grandpa，grandma，dad，mum and me. I like my living room.

【设计说明】 激起学生对温暖的家的爱和美好向往,为下一步的输出做好准备。

Activity 2：Talk about your home

A. Discuss and make dialogues in groups of four.

T：What's in your home? Let's talk with your partners.

> **Talk about your home**
>
> A：Look at my picture. This is the _____.
>
> B：Wow! Your _____ is really nice/great/good ... !
>
> A：Thanks. There *is/are* ...
>
> C：There *is* a/an _____.
>
> D：There *are* _____s.
>
> ...
>
> A：Please come to my home.
>
> B/C/D：OK!

B. Perform before the whole class.

【设计说明】 分享班级孩子的房间,极易吸引学生的注意力。学生在展示过程中,能够巩固和拓展对话的内容。

六、作业设计 （1 min）

1. Listen to the recording and read the dialogue on p51.

2. Talk about your photo with your friends and give a presentation next time.

【设计说明】 听读录音能够及时巩固所学知识。对话即是交际,学习是为了交流,课后与朋友谈论照片正是体现了"学以致用",而下节课上台展示则体现了课堂的连贯性和循环性。

七、板书设计

【设计说明】 语言学习的最终目的是提高学生的综合语用能力。教师按照课堂进展的

Talk about the pictures

PEP 5 U5 B Let's talk

picture

picture

picture

boy girl

There is a/an..
It is pretty/...

There are... s....
My... can draw...
My ... have a garden...

There are **so many**....

grandparents'   so many
in front of   lots of...

顺序逐步呈现图片和关键词、句,由"点"到"面"串联出本课的谈话脉络,能够帮助学生更好地梳理本课所学,帮助他们更好地输出,最终实现语言的综合运用。

八、 教学反思

本节课属于小学高年级英语对话教学课。教师在教授单词、词组以及句型的同时,还应注重培养学生的观察能力和思维品质。本节课中,教师灵活整合文本,基于教材内在的情境创设了多样化的教学活动和学习方式,引发学生思考,在师生真实交流中促进了学生能力的发展。

(一) 灵活整合文本,提升学生综合语用能力

在本节课中,教师能灵活整合单元文本,将教材内容进行"重新排序",在环环相扣的教学情境中(Zhang Peng's photo(A Talk), Pictures in the living room(B Try), Father's pictures and photo of grandparents' garden(B Talk), Students' photos)渗透新知识,引导学生学习和拓展新知识,使学生的学习既有趣又高效。

(二) 开展多种学习方式,促进学生能力发展

在本节课中,通过开展自主学习、小组合作、全班分享等多种学习方式,学生真实参与了课堂过程,展示了自我,张扬了个性。例如,教师在教授本课语言重点 There be 句型时,没有直接阐述语法要点,而是让学生开展自主学习,通过对比 There is/are ... 的异同,让学生在"我发现我解决"中,促进其观察、对比、总结等能力的发展。

(教学设计者:温州市双潮小学 郑珍珍)

Oxford English Book 3 M3U1 Welcome to my school

Hello! I'm Xia Zhen from Wenzhou Oujiang Primary School. It's my pleasure to share my lesson plan with you all. The lesson type is listening and speaking, which is from *Oxford English* Book 3 Module 3 *Places and Activities* Unit 1 *My School*. My presentation consists of five parts.

I. Analysis

Students have learnt the sentence patterns: "*What's this/that? Is this/that ...?*" and their corresponding answers: "*It's a/an ...*" and "*Yes/No*" in the second semester of Grade 1. It has laid a solid foundation for today's lesson. The lesson I'm going to present is the second period of Unit 1. In the previous period, students have studied the key words to identify different places in a school. The language focus is to understand the meanings of wh-questions (*Where's ...? This is ... ; What's this/that? It's the ...*) and use them to find out the information of the places they are looking for.

My students are in Grade 3. They have shown great interest in imitating and acting. After 2 years' of English learning, they have cultivated quite good habits of listening, speaking and reading. They can understand simple English dialogues and passages with the help of pictures and videos. They are willing to complete a simple task in English in real life. Considering their characteristics, I've designed several communicative activities they like to practice the language.

II. Statement

The learning objectives are as follows:

1) Communicative competence. First, by the end of this lesson, students will be able to understand two wh-questions in the context of the school and talk about it freely. They will understand the difference between "this" and "that". Second, they can comprehend the general idea of the dialogue, read and role-play it with the right pronunciation and intonation.

2) Cognitive and thinking ability. Students' understanding and analyzing ability will be improved during the learning process and they will be able to apply what they have learnt in the class to direct the way.

3) Social-cultural awareness. Students will find out the beauty of their school and evoke their love for it.

In order to achieve the objectives better, two micro-videos are made for lead-in and extension. An iPad and a while-learning worksheet are also used during the class. For my students, understanding the difference between "this" and "that" and using them properly will be the most difficult.

III. Description

The whole lesson can be divided into three stages: 1) warming-up & revision, 2) presentation & practice, 3) consolidation & extension.

At the beginning of the first stage, my students and I will sing a song together, which is named *On the way to school* to warm up the learning environment. Then I will ask them to guess the places I describe in order to review words. For instance, *there are many books. We can read picture books. We can read story books. What's that?* They may answer: *It's the library.* It aims to let students get as much language input as possible.

The second stage is presentation & practice. It contains 5 steps. They are *Let's try, Let's listen, Let's choose, Let's say* and *Let's wrap it up.* For the first step *Let's try,* students will watch a micro-video and answer my question: "Where's Miss Huang's classroom?" Miss Huang is a new teacher in our school. With the help of micro-video and real-life context, they can easily find the answer to the question "Where is ...?" After learning how to answer, it goes to the study of how to ask. I will ask students "where is the hall?", and then ask them to point out the right picture on the screen and click it to magnify the picture. After my demonstration, I will show an iPad to a student and ask him/her to answer my question *"Where is the library?"* so that others can learn from him or her. By using the iPad, students needn't leave or go back to the seats. It can save time. Meanwhile, they first listen to my explanations about "Where's ...?" "This is ... "; and then, they will learn from the demonstrations by me and their classmates; Finally they will understand the question "Where's ... " and they will be able to either ask or answer correctly.

The second step *Let's listen* brings the real-life situation to the students. It's a transition from new teacher Miss Huang to the new student Peter, the characters on the book. Students will be asked to listen to the recording for *Say and act* on p27 and do Task 1 *Listen and choose* on the worksheet. While filling the blanks of places, they will have a general idea of the dialogue.

The third step *Let's choose* deals with the language focus. Students will listen to the recording again and answer my question: "Where's Peter's classroom?" There are four options for them to choose. As I present picture A, C, D and B, they will study the negative and positive answers to the question: *Is this the classroom?* respectively. Then they will be asked to sort the four pictures out into 2 groups according to "this" and "that". [They will observe carefully and group them in line with different positions of Miss Huang and Peter.] By the door: *this*; away from the door: *that*. In this process, the learning strategy — learning by observation will be developed. They will classify the four pictures into 2 groups accroding to "this" and "that".

The next one *Let's say* will put what the students leant in the third step *Let's choose* into practice. I will ask the students to choose one map of Task 2 on the worksheet and make a dialogue in pairs, for pair work can maximize the involvement of all the students. Afterwards, I will invite several pairs to act out in front of the class so that their speaking and acting skills will be practiced.

At the end of the second stage, it's a brief sum-up called *Let's wrap it up*. I will play the recording for the third time, and let students read after it, while encouraging them to take notes on the intonation, stress and liaison.

Now it comes to the third stage — consolidation and extension. In this stage, there are two steps. Step 1, students will enjoy a micro-video of their school with lots of pictures of what they've done at school, so as to evoke their love for it. Step 2 is *Let's act*. It provides them with three scenarios for practical application. They are, Scene 1, Lisa is joining a singing contest; Scene 2, Tim's brother Tom wants to use the toilet; Scene 3, Danny is joining a sports meeting. Instead of telling them where to go for, I will advise them to associate with daily life to choose the right floor map. Taking Lisa's situation as an example, I'll lead them to create the dialogue step by step, and finally let them act it out in pairs.

IV. Exposition

This is the layout of the board writing. The title is on the top and the floor map is under it. The dialogue we're learning about in this lesson is in the center of the board which aims to highlight the key sentences. The complete passage is displayed so that they can get the exact words to say, which is like a walking stick for them.

And here is the homework. Homework 1 is to listen to the recording and read the dialogue on p27. It's necessary for students to go over what they have learnt after class. All of them can make it. An optional homework is to draw a map of their school and introduce it to their parents or friends. The students are encouraged to complete this task with the help of worksheet. It can apply what they have learnt in class into real life using.

Ⅴ．Reflection

To sum up, my plan has two shining points.

First, the design of the activities or tasks embodies students' learning process, i. e. from known to unknown, from easy to complex. From the worksheet, we can see the difficulty steps up progressively: Task 1, listen and choose, Task 2, choose and say, Task 3, say and act.

Second, students learn to use the language in life-like and real-life situations. For instance, while learning the key structure "Where's …?" "This is …", they intend to associate it with the situation of their new teacher Miss Huang. And they are encouraged to put language into use in the context of the three given scenarios. Undoubtedly, these diverse situations will greatly help with the learning process.

Well, that is all for my presentation. Many thanks for your attention.

（说课稿撰写者：温州市鹿城区瓯江小学　夏臻）

附：教学设计

一、教学背景

1. 教材分析

本节课的教学内容选自（上海版试用本）《牛津英语》三年级上册第三模块 *Places and Activities*，第一单元 *My School* 的第 2 课时 Say and act，即对话表演课。本课时，学生将在教材提供的 school 语境中，熟练掌握句型 What's this/that? Is this/that …? 及其回答：It's the … 和 Yes, it is. /No, it isn't. 并运用对话 Where's …? This is …。

2. 学情分析

学生在一年级上册第 4 模块（该模块为选学模块），已能够初步运用句型 What's this/that? Is this/that …? 及其简要回答：It's a/an … 和 Yes. /No. 为本课的灵活运用奠定了基础。三年级的学生活泼好动，善于模仿，喜爱表演，对学习英语有着浓厚的兴趣。经过两年的英语学习，学生能看懂简单的英语视频，乐于用英语完成生活中的简单任务。教师可以充分利用学生的这些特点，以生活实际为导向，组织学生进行对话表演，学以致用。

二、 教学目标

1. 语言交际目标：

（1）能够听、说、读，并在情境中运用句型 Where's . . . ? This is . . . What's this/that? It's the . . . 并结合已学句型 We can . . . 对学校场所及开展的活动进行简单描述；区分指示代词 this 和 that，并灵活运用。

（2）能理解对话大意，按照正确的语音、语调朗读对话，并进行角色扮演。

2. 思维认知目标：

（1）能通过比较分析 this 和 that 的不同用法，提升理解与分析层次的认知能力。

（2）能够在真实的语用情境中，结合地点图示，运用目标句型完成地点指引，提高运用层次的认知能力。

3. 社会文化目标：

在 My school 的语境下，通过描述和问答，感受学校的美丽，体验校园生活的快乐。

三、 教学重难点

1. 教学重点：

在语境中理解并运用 Where's . . . ? This is . . . What's this/that? It's the . . . 等句型进行简单问答。

2. 教学难点：

指示代词 this 和 that 的区分及运用。

四、 教学准备

多媒体课件、微课视频、希沃一体机、平板电脑（教师用）、学习单。

五、 教学过程

Stage 1 Warm-up & revision (5 mins)

Step 1 Sing a song: *On the way to school*

On the way to school today

I met a little friend

Joining hands we went along, went along, went along

Joining hands we went along

And this is how we went

We tramp/walk/skip/hop/jump along to school

Step 2 Let's guess

Guess what places they are.

T：There are many books. We can read picture books. We can read story books. What's that?

Ss：(It's the library.)

T：There are many desks and chairs. We can learn English. We can have classes. What's that?

Ss：(It's the classroom.)

T：There are slides and swings. We can play football. We can play basketball. What's that?

Ss：(It's the playground.)

T：We can sing. We can dance. We can play the piano. What's that?

Ss：(It's the hall.)

Stage 2 Presentation & practice (20 mins)

Step 1 Let's try

Activity 1：Try to find Miss Huang's classroom in the video

T：Miss Huang is a new teacher in our school. She is new here. Let's watch a video and find：
Where's Miss Huang's classroom?

A. Class 5，Grade 1.   B. Class 5，Grade 3.

Activity 2：Practise the sentence pattern：This is the＋place

T：(PPT shows the picture of classroom)This is the classroom. Read after me.

Ss：...

T：(PPT shows the picture of library)This is ...

Ss：the library.

T：(PPT shows the picture of hall)This ...

Ss：is the hall.

T：(PPT shows the picture of school)

Ss：This is the school.

(Then the slides will show the pictures of the playground and toilet，and students say the whole sentence accordingly.)

说出整个句子,体现了学生"学"的过程。

Activity 3:Learn the sentence pattern:Where's the . . .? This is the . . .

T:Where is the hall?

(Teacher clicks the picture of the hall and the picture magnifies.)

Ss:This is the hall.

T:Now,where is the library?

(Teacher shows the iPad to Student 1 to click the right picture.)

S1:This is the library.

T:And where is the playground?

S2:(Clicks the picture of playground) This is the playground.

(After several rounds,students will be asked to ask and answer by themselves.)

【设计说明】 学完 Where's the . . .? 的答句,本步骤学习该问句。利用希沃软件中课件与 iPad 同步的功能,点击 iPad 图片,电脑上的图片同时放大(诠释 This is the . . . 句型),如此操控 PPT 课件,可以免去学生离开座位、跑上讲台、再归位的时间,使课堂环节更为流畅。同时,先由教师提问地点,个别学生示范回答,促进同伴间相互学习,然后放手让学生互相提问,问句和答句均被练习到。

Step 2 Let's listen

Activity 1:Let's guess who the boy is

T:After talking about the new teacher Miss Huang,here comes a friend. Let's listen and guess who he is.

【设计说明】 听力训练是一个循序渐进的过程,不仅要"听"课本,也要"听"辅助的细节信息,抓住一切可以给学生输入语段的机会,使其"浸润"其中,不断积累。

Activity 2:Listen and choose

Listen to the recording for "Say and act" on p27 of the Student's Book and do *Task 1: Listen and choose* on the worksheet (as follows).

Listen and choose	
A. classroom B. library C. hall D. school E. playground F. toilet	A:Good morning. I'm new here. 　Where's my _____? B:This is your classroom. A:What's that? B:It's the _____. A:Is this the library? B:No. It's the _____. A:Is that the _____? B:Yes, it is. A:Thank you. B:You're welcome.

【设计说明】 第一遍泛听,整体感知语篇和语境。语言学习,听力先行。学生根据课文录

音,选择填写相关单词。

Step 3 Let's choose

Activity 1：Listen again and answer the question

T：Look at the pictures and listen to the recording again. Try to answer my question. Where's Peter's classroom? There are four options for you to choose.

A
Is this the classroom?
No, it isn't.

B
Is this the classroom?
Yes, it is.

C
Is that the classroom?
No, it isn't.

D
Is that the classroom?
Yes, it is.

【设计说明】 第二遍精听,再次感知文本,并深入到细节,回答提问：Where's Peter's classroom? 随着 A、C、D 和 B 四幅图的呈现,逐步教授 Is this/that ...? 的否定回答 No, it isn't. 和肯定回答 Yes, it is.

Activity 2：Sort the pictures into 2 groups according to *this* and *that*

【设计说明】 让学生自己去发现 Is this ... 和 Is that ... 的不同用法,在观察中学习：this, Miss Huang 和 Peter 站在所谈论的场馆边上；that,他俩离场馆要远些。

Step 4 Let's say

Choose one map of Task 2 on the worksheet and practise in pairs.

【设计说明】 马上运用上个环节刚学习的知识点：this 和 that 的区分,完成练习,巩固所学。同时,同桌操练,扩大参与面。

Step 5 Let's wrap it up

Listen to the recording and imitate it. Pay attention to the tones，stresses and liaisons.

【设计说明】 第三次通篇精听,并模仿朗读。学生一边精听录音,一边和教师一起判断语调、重音以及是否存在连读,使用相关符号,把学习要点记录在课本上,即小结阶段性学习成果,为下一阶段的创编运用打下基础。

Stage 3　Consolidation & extension（10 mins）

Step 1　Enjoy a micro-video

Activity 1：Watch a video of their school life

T：So much for Peter's school. Do you like it?

Ss：（Yes，we do.）

T：What about our school? Let's enjoy the micro-video：

> **Narrator：**
>
> This is our school. It's big and nice. There are many great places. This is the hall. We can sing and dance here. This is the library. There are many books. We can read picture books and story books. This is our classroom. We can learn English and have other classes. And that's the playground. There are slides and swings. We can play basketball，football and practise Taekwondo there. Do you like our school?

【设计说明】　以学生在校学习、运动、游戏、娱乐的真实图片为背景，并配以适度的英文解说和感染人心的音乐，使其燃起对学校的热爱之情以及主人翁意识。

Step 2　Let's act

Activity 1：Get to know the scenarios

T：There are some guests coming to our school. Can you be a warm host?

Ss：（Yes，I can.）

T：Look here，this is Lisa. She is coming to our school for a singing contest. Where is she going to ?

S1：（The hall.）

T：Hello. I'm new here. Where's the hall? （T points at the maps on the PPT.）

S1：（S1 points to Map A and says *this is the hall*.）

T：What's this ? （T points to the library.）

S1：It's the library.

T：We can ...

S2：We can read books.

T：What's that ? （T points to the playground.）

S2：It's the library. We can play football.

T：Thank you.

S1：You're welcome.

【设计说明】　学以致用，将书本所学运用到生活中。教师创设了3个真实的语用情境：一、外校的学生来本校参加唱歌比赛；二、生活中常见的找厕所情景；三、外校友人来参加运动

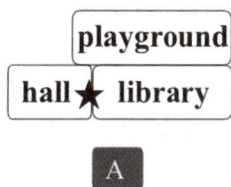

A

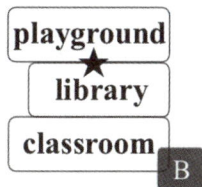

B

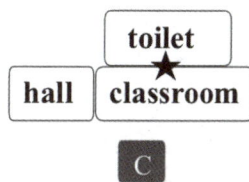

C

会；均不是指定学生问某个地点，而是根据具体的情况，结合生活中的地点图示，通过教师和学生的示范，引导其加以区分运用。

Activity 2：Act out the scenario in pairs

T：Now，look at your worksheet，Task 3. Work in pairs. Fill in the blanks with the words in word bank. And then act out your dialogue.

A：Hello. I'm new here. Where's the _____？
B：This is the _____. We can _____.
A：What's this?
B：It's the _____. We can _____.
A：What's that?
B：It's the _____. We can _____.
A：Thank you.
B：You're welcome.

Word bank：

playground；classroom；toilet；hall；library；dance；play football；skip；run；play basketball；sing；read books；read and write；have classes . . .

【设计说明】　发挥孩子爱表演的天性，让其演一演，巩固和拓展对话学习。

六、　作业布置

1. Listen to the recording and read the dialogue on P27.

2. Draw a map of our school and introduce it to your parents or friends.

【设计说明】　学生需要及时复习、巩固学习内容，所以作业 1 要求全体学生听、读课文第 27 页；而作业 2 的要求稍高一些，学有余力的孩子可在学习单的帮助下，向父母或朋友介绍自己的学校，学以致用。

七、　板书设计

【设计说明】　三年级的学生对语调、重音和连读的敏感度还是稍显欠缺，需要教师反复强调；将其出示在板书中，确保学生能正确标记在自己的课本上，以备反复练习。需要特别指出的是，板书上并没有挖空，只是在需要替换的词条上做了下划线处理，目的是照顾到后 20% 的学生。

3A　M3U1 Welcome to my school（p2）

playground

hall　★　library

A: Hello. I'm new here. Where's the hall?

B: This is the hall. We can sing and dance.

A: What's this?

B: It's the library. We can read books.

A: What's that?

B: It's the playground. We can run and skip rope.

A: Thank you.

B: You're welcome.

附：学习单

Welcome to my school 学习单

Task1：Listen and choose （听一听，选一选）

A.classroom

B. library

C.hall

D. school

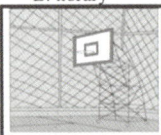

E. playground

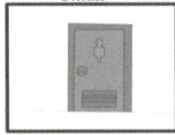

F. toilet

A: Good morning. I'm new here.
Where's my _____?
B: This is your classroom.
A: What's that?
B: It's the _____.
A: Is this the library?
B: No. It's the _____.
A: Is that the _____?
B: Yes, it is.
A: Thank you.
B: You're welcome.

Task2：Choose and say （选一选，说一说：选择一幅图，同桌说一说 ）

playground

hall　★　library

A

playground　★

library

classroom

B

toilet

★

hall　classroom

C

★ You are here.

A: What's this ?
B: It's the _____.
　We can _____.

A: What's that ?
B: It's the _____.
　We can _____.

Task 3：Say and act （说一说，演一演：选择一个场景，四人小组演一演）

A: Hello. I'm new here. Where's the _____?

B: This is the _____. We can _____.

A: What's this?

B: It's the _____.We can _____.

A: What's that?

B: It's the _____.We can _____.

A: Thank you.

B: You're welcome.

> **Words bank:**
> playground；classroom；
> toilet；hall；library；
> play football；skip；
> play basketball；run；
> sing；dance；read books；
> read and write；
> have classes ...

八、教学反思

本节课上，该教师以 Welcome to my school 为题，采取课中学习单助学、同伴互学、小组合作等形式，由易到难，循序渐进地发展学生的语言运用能力，基本完成了本节课的教学任务。反思本节课教学，我们可以得到的启示有以下几个方面。

1. 关注教材解读，创设整体语境。

以往的对话教学设计，一直苦于情境的创设。而本节课以新教师寻找教室为始，引出课文人物新生 Peter 对各个场所的询问，最后要求学生用自己的话为校外友人介绍本校的相关情况，从生活中来，又回到生活中去，一气呵成，使学生在统整的语境中完成词汇、句型的学习和操练。

2. 关注学生活动，提高思维品质。

本次教学设计中，该教师特别关注英语课堂中思维品质的培养。从热身活动开始，学生需要调动思维，链接已学词汇；任务中，学生细心辨察 this 和 that 图片的区别；实际运用阶段，学生根据不同情境，思考选用具体的图示与对话。在文本教学推进中，通过观察、比较、分析等学习活动，使思维之花"绽放"于英语课堂。

（教学设计者：温州市鹿城区瓯江小学　夏臻）

说课案例三（词汇课）

PEP 4 Unit 3 Weather Part A Let's learn

Good afternoon，everyone! I'm Zhong Yuhan from Oujiang Primary School. It's my great honor to present my lesson plan here. The lesson I'll present is from PEP 4 Unit 3 *Weather* Part A *Let's learn*.

微课

I. Analysis

The lesson type is vocabulary learning, and the theme of this unit is about "weather". The purpose of this lesson is to learn the key words "cold, cool, warm, hot" in a weather report and to use these 3-skilled words in the sentence structure "It's ... in ..." to describe the weather of a city. Besides, the words "cold" and "hot" have appeared in the first period of this unit. It is easier for the students to learn these two words in this lesson. *Let's chant* can be used as an activity for students to practise the key points.

As for the students in Grade 4 of primary school, they have learned a lot of vocabularies so they can learn an unknown word with the help of the known words. They are willing to work cooperatively. However, some of them haven't learned a lot about dressing and it might be a little difficult for them to make a new chant or make a WeChat message. But group members can help.

II. Statement

Based on the analysis above, I will set the learning objectives as follows. As for communicative competence: firstly, students will be able to understand the meaning of "weather report", and pronounce it correctly by the end of this class. Secondly, they will be able to listen, speak and read these words, and can use "It's ... in ..." to describe the weather of a city. Thirdly, they will be able to understand and read after the chant together, and make a new chant in groups. As for cognitive and thinking ability: firstly, students will be able to generalize the rules of pronunciation by comparison; secondly, they will promote their cooperative learning strategies through pair work and group work. As for social-cultural awareness: firstly, students will know the weather distribution in China and be interested in the weather in daily life. Besides, they will be able to offer suggestions on dressing according to the weather report after class.

As it is a vocabulary lesson, the language focus is to enable students to know the pronunciation, the form and the meaning of the key words in a real context by group work. However, it's difficult for the students to tell the weather according to the given temperatures and use "It's ... in ..." to describe the weather of a city.

In order to deal with the objectives above, the whole lesson will adopt the 3P model including presentation, practice and production.

III. Description

Now I will show my teaching procedures. The whole lesson will be divided into four stages. They are lead-in, presentation, practice and production.

In the stage of lead-in, there are two activities. In activity one, the students will enjoy a video which tells them that different weather decides their dressing in a day. The video leads in the topic of the lesson and attracts students' attention. In Activity 2, students are led to read the word "weather" with the help of some familiar words, such as brother, mother, father with "ther" sound, and head, sweater, bread with "ea"/e/sound. This activity aims to break through the difficulty of pronunciation and help students to learn the words more efficiently.

In the second stage — presentation, there are six activities which will help the students learn the key words step by step. Firstly, in order for students to have an overall perception of the weather report, I will ask them to listen to the weather report once and fill in the blank orally. Students should listen and identify the word "warm". They learn the word "warm" and use "It's warm in . . . " to consolidate the word.

After listening, here comes Activity 2. Students have to read the weather report by themselves and circle the words about weather. Then one student will be asked to circle the words on SEEWO which is an all-in-all machine. Thus, the students will pay attention to the form of the key words.

In Activity 3, students are asked to learn the pronunciation of the key words in pairs with the help of the familiar words in order to deal with the pronunciation. Such as old for cold; school for cool; dog, fox for hot. Students can not only master the way of learning words but also learn to cooperate with others.

In Activity 4, students will read after the weather report to check the pronunciation of the key words. Meanwhile, students will know how to describe the temperature in English.

In Activity 5, I will write down these words and cities on the blackboard: Harbin, Lhasa, Beijing, Hong Kong. The students are required to reconstruct the weather report by using "It's . . . in . . . ". It will help students to consolidate the key words and sentence structure. While transferring the structure, students' thinking quality will be enhanced.

To learn a word is to learn its form, pronunciation and meaning. So, in the last activity of this stage, I will show them the temperature range of cold, cool, warm and hot. So the students will use the words correctly.

Now, we come to practice. There are three activities. In Activity 1, I will present a temperature map for students. They should respond quickly and make a sentence in the sentence pattern "It's . . . in . . . ". For example, I will present "Xinjiang, 13 degrees", the students will say:"It's cool in Xinjiang. " Then they are asked to chant with the tape recording together. The rhyming chant can further consolidate the key words and make learning more interesting. In the next activity, the students are led to make a new chant in a group. I have designed two levels of tasks for them in order for all the students to participate in the class. And the top students can help others in a group by cooperative activities.

The last stage is production. There are two activities. In Activity 1, I will present a temperature map with several cities for the students. They will talk about the weather of China today and give some suggestions on dressing. While looking at the map, students will know more about the geography and weather of China. Then I will show four friends on the same map for them, they are in different cities of China. Students are required to work in groups and send a WeChat message. The message should include the weather information and the dressing suggestions. WeChat is close to students' life, so they are willing to talk more.

IV. Exposition

My blackboard design is simple but clear. On the left side, there are the key words about weather. And on the right, there are some names of the big cities. The sentence structure "It's ... in ..." is the language focus of this lesson. My blackboard design can help students to consolidate what they've learned in this lesson and it can help them to give the presentation.

Finally let's come to today's homework. Firstly, listen to the tape recording and read after the words and chant on Page 25. Secondly, check the weather report and send the WeChat message to the teacher which includes the weather condition and dressing suggestions. The first task is regular one which aims to consolidate what they've learned in the class and the second one enables students to apply what they've learned into practice.

V. Reflection

To sum up, I think there are two shining points in my lesson plan. Firstly, I have designed several activities to lead students to learn the words from three aspects — pronunciation, form and meaning step by step. Secondly, I make full use of the text. I combine *Let's learn* and *Let's chant* together to enrich the topic and enhance the students' comprehensive language competence. Giving suggestions on dressing reflects the humanistic concern of the class. Meanwhile, WeChat will be used in the lesson, which activates students' learning passion.

That's all for my lesson plan presentation. Thank you for your attention.

（说课稿撰写者：温州市鹿城区瓯江小学　钟好涵）

一、教学背景

1. 教材分析

本课的教学内容选自人教版《英语》四年级下册*Unit 3 Weather* 第2课时词汇课。该教学语篇主题为 weather report,文本的功能句 It's ... in ...能为学生介绍不同地方的天气提供句型框架。本节课的目标词汇为 cold,cool,hot,warm,此类词汇的掌握有助于学生描述天气状况。此外,Let's chant 环节不仅可以用于巩固操练核心词汇,还能丰富话题内容,提供穿衣建议,体现人文情怀。

2. 学情分析

四年级的学生经过一年半的英语学习,已有一定的词汇积累,在教师的引导下,能够借助已知词汇的拼读规则学习新词汇。他们知道如何进行小组合作,并乐于参与小组合作学习。然而,大部分学生没有学过衣服类单词,编歌谣与发微信消息的活动对于他们会有难度,但是小组成员可以相互帮助,共同进步。

二、教学目标

1. 语言交际目标:

(1)能在语境中理解 weather report 的意思,并正确发音;能听、说、认读单词:warm,cool,cold,hot,并能在语境中正确使用功能句 It's ... in ...来介绍不同地方的天气状况。

(2)能在图片的帮助下听懂并跟读歌谣;能够替换关键词创编新的歌谣。

2. 思维认知目标:

(1)通过对比跟读单词发音,提升判断分析能力。

(2)通过同桌合作学习、小组合作学习等方式,提高学生的协作策略。

3. 社会文化目标:

了解中国天气状况的分布特点,关心日常天气状况,并根据不同的天气给予他人不同的穿衣建议。

三、教学重难点

1. 教学重点

能掌握词汇 warm,cool,cold,hot,weather 的音、形、义,并正确运用句型 It's ... in ...来介绍不同地方的天气状况。

2. 教学难点

能根据给出的不同温度区间,判断 cold 等描述天气的单词词意,并用功能句 It's ...

in ... 介绍不同地方的天气状况。

四、 教学准备

多媒体课件、微课视频、希沃一体机、教学卡片。

五、 教学过程

Stage 1   Lead-in (3 mins)

Step 1   Enjoy a video

Enjoy a video which shows that different weather conditions decide our dressing in a day.

【设计说明】   导入话题,让学生提前感知真实的天气预报,引发学生的求知欲望,快速进入学习的状态。

Narrator：

Weather decides my dressing in a day. In a cold day，I wear a hat，a scarf and a pair of gloves. In a hot day，I wear a cap and a pair of sunglasses. In a cool or warm day，I wear a coat and a pair of jeans.

Step 2   Read and learn

Pronounce the word *weather* with the help of familiar words.

T：It's hot in Wenzhou, so I wear a T-shirt today. Our dressing depends on ... （The teacher shows students the title of the lesson. ）

Ss：...

T：Can you read these words?

  （Ss read *head*，*sweater*，*bread*，*breakfast*. ）

T：So "ea" says ...

Ss：/e/.

T：How about these words?

  （Ss read *brother*，*mother*，*father*，*together*. ）

T："ther" says ...

  Ss：/ðə/

  （T points to the word *weather*. ）

T：How can we read this word?

Ss：Weather.

【设计说明】   通过学生熟悉的单词的发音,引导学生拼读出单词 weather,为接下来的词汇学习做铺垫。

Stage 2　Presentation (12 mins)

Activity 1：Listen and learn

Read the phrase *weather report* correctly，watch a video of the weather report and fill in the blank orally.

> Good morning，this is the weather report. It's _____ in Beijing today.
>
> Harbin，5℃，cold.
>
> Hong Kong，30℃，hot.
>
> Lhasa，15℃，cool.

T：It's warm in Beijing today. Which city is warm too? (The teacher writes "It's . . . in . . . " and "warm" on the blackboard.)

Ss：It's warm in . . .

【设计说明】　让学生整体感知 weather report 的语篇。视频呈现直观清晰,学生在反复观看、聆听答案的过程中,掌握单词 warm 的"音""形""义"。教师指导学生正确发音,并让学生运用 It's . . . in . . . 回答问题,巩固单词的发音,熟悉功能句的运用。

Activity 2：Read and circle

Circle the other words about weather in the weather report on SEEWO (all-in-one machine).

【设计说明】　学生到一体机上圈单词极大地调动了大部分学生的学习积极性,且由于知觉的选择性,学生会格外关注所圈单词的"形"。

Activity 3：Learn to pronounce

Work in pairs and learn the pronunciation of the following words.

A	B
<u>o</u>ld	c<u>o</u>ld
d<u>o</u>g f<u>o</u>x	h<u>o</u>t
sch<u>oo</u>l	c<u>oo</u>l

T：Now please work in pairs, read the words in A and try to read these new words in B.

【设计说明】　单词的记忆和拼读是学好英语的关键。本活动中,学生利用旧知进行迁移,在遵循拼读规则的基础上学习四个目标词汇,并在合作中相互帮助,提升合作学习能力。

Activity 4：Listen and check

Listen to the weather report and follow it.

【设计说明】　课文的原版语音是学生学习英文单词正确发音的最佳途径,学生能在跟读过程中了解温度的表达方法。

Activity 5：Reconstruct and say

Reconstruct the weather report by using "It's . . . in . . .".

(The teacher sticks the flashcard of key words and four cities on the blackboard.)

Good morning，this is the weather report. It's _____ in Beijing today.

It's _____ in _____.

It's _____ in _____.

【设计说明】 转换句型能有效巩固词与句的运用。

Activity 6：Guess and know

Guess the temperature ranges of cold/cool/warm/hot weather.

(The teacher shows students the correct temperature ranges：cold≤10℃；10℃＜cool≤15℃；15℃＜warm≤25℃；hot＞25℃.)

【设计说明】 该环节解决了词汇的"义"，学生明确温度区间后，在表达运用上会更加严谨准确。

Stage 3 Practice (8 mins)

Activity 1：Respond quickly

Give a complete sentence with the structure "It's . . . in . . . " according to the information given by the teacher.

T：Xinjiang，13℃.

S1：It's cool in Xinjiang.

T：Hainan，37℃.

S2：It's hot in Hainan.

【设计说明】 该活动主要有两个目的：一是理解上一环节的气温度数与四个目标词的关系；二是通过快速反应活动，培养学生推理、思辨等思维能力。

Activity 2：Learn to chant

Listen to the chant first and then chant together.

(The teacher shows students some pictures in Harbin and a girl from "Let's chant".)

T：Where is she?

Ss：(She is in Harbin.)

T：How's the weather in Harbin?

Ss：(It's cold in Harbin.)

Let's chant

Brrr，it's cold.

It's cold outside.

Put on a hat.

Cold，bye-bye!

Mmm! It's warm!

It's warm inside!

Take off your shoes.

It feels so nice.

【设计说明】 该活动中有韵律的节奏说唱,强化单词的音义匹配训练旨在操练已学词汇并增加课堂的趣味性。

Activity 3：Make a chant

Talk about the weather in summer and give dressing suggestions.

T：It's hot in Wenzhou. Is it cold outside in Wenzhou?

S1：No，it's hot outside.

T：Can you give me some suggestions if I go outside?

S1：... (Students are led to give different ideas. The teacher writes the ideas on the blackboard.)

T：Is it warm inside?

S2：No，it's cool inside.

T：Yes，we can take off the sunglasses and cap inside. Anything else?

Sn：...

T：Please work in groups of four，choose one task and make a new chant for summer in Wenzhou.

Make a chant Tips:小组合作，根据板书编一首新 chant

Wow, it's hot.
It's hot outside.
_____.
I feel good.
Mmm, it's cool.
It's cool inside.
_____.
I like summer.

Wow, it's hot.
It's hot outside.
_____.
_____.
Mmm, it's cool.
It's cool inside.
_____.
_____.

【设计说明】 分层任务的设计具有一定的挑战性,旨在让每个学生都能参与到课堂活动中,且在小组合作中,通过事物特征的描述,培养学生概括分析能力。活动中,优等生帮助后进生,带动学习。

Stage 4　Production (12 mins)

Activity 1：Know the weather in China

Look at a map full of cities with their temperatures，talk about them and give suggestions accordingly.

T：Look，this is a weather report map，which city is cold today? It's cold in Harbin today. Anything else?

S1：It's ... in ... today.

T：If I were in Harbin now，can you offer some suggestions?

S1：(Put on your hat.)

T：Which city is cool/warm/hot?

Ss：It's ... in ... today. (Students give suggestions accordingly.)

T：It's cool and cold in northern China，but things are opposite in southern China.　It's ...

Ss：(Warm and hot.)

【设计说明】 学生在该环节巩固了核心词汇以及句型的运用,并通过中国地图的直观呈现,了解中国天气分布特点。

Activity 2：Care about the friends

Work in groups of four and give suggestions for Zhang Peng，Mike，Sarah and Amy.

T：Look，my friends are travelling now.　Where are they?

Ss：(Urumchi，Sanya，Liaoning，Hangzhou ...)

T：Please work in groups of four，choose one person and send a WeChat message to him/her.　The message should include the weather and the dressing suggestions.

| It's ____ in _____. _____. @Zhang Peng |
| It's ____ in _____. _____. @Mike |
| It's ____ in _____. _____. @Sarah |
| It's ____ in _____. _____. @Amy |

【设计说明】 微信聊天贴近学生生活,让学生会更乐于开口说。小组合作输出,让孩子体会到合作学习的快乐,达到综合语用输出。

六、作业布置

1. Listen to the recording and read the words and chant on page 25.

2. Check the weather report and send Wechat message to teacher：

It's ＿＿ in＿＿＿. ＿＿＿＿＿.

【设计说明】 作业1为常规作业,要求学生倾听、跟读课文25页的录音,及时复习巩固学习内容;作业2为创新作业,结合时下学生熟悉的微信,让学生通过微信发送天气预报与穿衣建议给老师,学以致用。

七、 板书设计

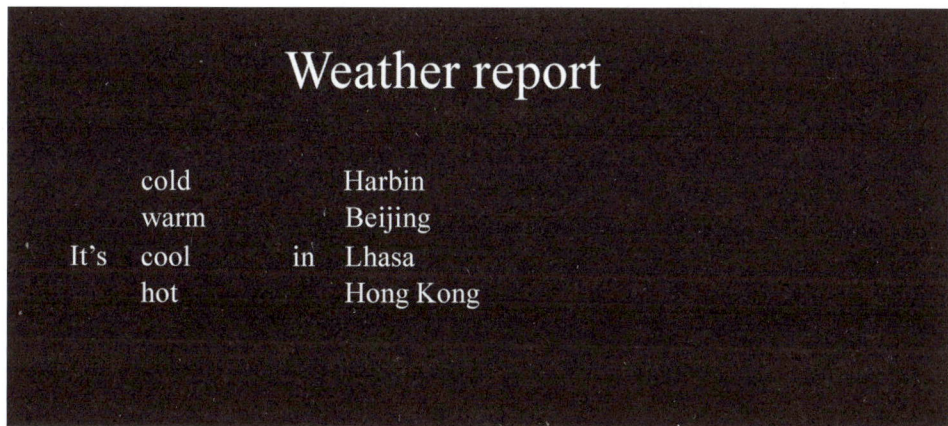

```
                    Weather report

               cold        Harbin
               warm        Beijing
      It's     cool    in  Lhasa
               hot         Hong Kong
```

【设计说明】 板书是教学目标的呈现,该板书清晰地呈现了本节课的语言知识目标。学生能够根据板书说出语段。

八、 教学反思

1. 合作学习词汇,落实"音""形""义"

本节课中,教师设计多种学习活动,循序渐进地引导学生从词汇的"音""形""义"三方面落实单词。比如,通过阅读圈出单词解决单词的"形",通过同桌合作学习解决单词的"音",通过学生观看生动形象的视频感知"义",并通过猜温度范围的活动解决单词的"义"。继而学生在接下来的练习巩固活动中不断巩固强化对核心词汇的"音""形""义"的认知,达到熟练运用。

2. 整合课本资源,体现人文关怀

笔者将Let's learn与Let's chant有机结合在一起,让Let's chant辅助词汇的学习,丰富话题,并提升学生的综合语言素养。学生不仅可以用功能句It's . . . in . . . 来介绍天气,还能根据天气给予穿衣建议,体现人文关怀。与此同时,笔者引入贴近学生生活的微信聊天,激发了学生的学习热情,让学生学以致用;并将课堂内容延伸到课后作业,学生看天气预报后发送微信给老师,从中能体会到英语学习的乐趣与作用。

（教学设计者：温州市鹿城区瓯江小学　钟妤涵）

PEP 5 Unit 5 There is a big bed. Part A Let's talk

微课

Good morning，everyone! I'm Zhou Peipei from Qin Yuan Primary School. It's my great honor to present my lesson plan here. The lesson is from PEP 5 Unit 5 *There is a big bed* Part A *Let's talk*.

Ⅰ. Analysis

The topic of this material is about "my room". It is a dialogue among Sarah，Mike and Zhang Peng when Sarah and Mike are visiting Zhang Peng's bedroom. They are talking about the things in Zhang Peng's room and also describing the positions of them. The purpose of this lesson is to learn the singular form of *There be* structure. Meanwhile，it's also a lesson to enlighten students on expressing their thoughts or feelings，such as *"Your room is really nice." "You look cool." "I like your bed."* and so on.

With the analysis of teaching material mentioned above，let me introduce my students. They are from Grade 5. They like songs，videos and role-plays and they are very active to air their opinions and do the role-plays. They have learned how to describe positions in Grade 4 and they are very familiar with today's topic — room. So it's not very difficult for them to learn *There be* structure after two years' English learning.

Ⅱ. Statement

After analyzing the basic information of this lesson，here come the teaching objectives.

For Communicative competence：Firstly，after the lesson，students will understand the meaning of this dialogue with the help of the pictures and the teacher. They will be able to use the new word *photo* and the new expression *there is* skillfully in real situations. Secondly，students will be able to use *"There is a/an ..."* to talk about the things and their positions in a place. They can read the dialogue confidently with correct pronunciation，intonation，stress，sense-group and act it out.

For Cognitive and thinking ability：Firstly，students will understand the new words and expressions with the help of the video made by the teacher. Secondly，students will improve their analyzing ability by doing predicting activity.

For Social-cultural awareness：Firstly，students will be willing to describe things and positions in English. Secondly，they will start to think about their own dream rooms in colours, the things in it and their positions.

III. Description

Here come my teaching procedures. There are three stages.

The first stage is revision and lead-in. This stage is made up of three activities. Students will firstly observe and describe the classmates and the teacher by using "*You look ...*", which will liven up the class atmosphere. And then they will sing a song together and think about rooms at home: *What are they? What do you often do in these rooms?* These three activities are mainly designed to help students review the words and lead to today's topic.

In the second stage, there are three steps with several activities. These steps are closely related to today's topic: talking about room.

Step 1 is about talking Amy's room. There are four activities. Firstly, students will watch the video and answer the questions: *What is the video about? Whose room is it?* According to the video, students will generally know the things in Amy's room and some students will be aware of how to use "*There is a/an ...*". Secondly, students will look at the picture of Amy's room and talk about the things in it. Through this activity, students will try to understand the meaning of the new word *photo*. And it also helps to emphasize the language focus of this class: to use the singular form of *There is* structure. Thirdly, students will chant together. It helps students to practice *There is* structure in time. Fourthly, I will ask students to share their feelings of Amy's room. And then students are asked to describe Amy's room in passage. This activity is designed to help students have a better understanding of *There is* structure.

Step 2 is about the learning of *Let's try* on P48. There are three activities. Firstly, students will look at the picture and pay attention to the things in Zhang Peng's room: a computer or a TV. Then they will listen to the recording carefully and tick the right answer on P48. After that, I will check the answer. This activity is designed to get them ready for the next task.

Step 3 is about the dialogue of *Let's talk*. There are three activities. With the help of *Let's try*, students have got some information of Zhang Peng's room. So, at the beginning, students will predict other things in Zhang Peng's room. Then they will listen to the recording and tick the things. Prediction before listening enables students to closely understand the general idea of the listening material. Secondly, students will watch the whole video once and answer three questions: *What's the bed like? What's the photo like? Where is the computer?* Thirdly, students will listen to the dialogue and mark the intonation. Through Activity 3, students' pronunciation and intonation will be better.

Now it comes to the last stage: Consolidation and production. There are two activities. Students will show the photos of their own rooms and they will work in pairs to make a new dialogue about their own rooms. This activity is used to arouse students' interest so that they will be involved into talking in English. And it also helps to use the singular form of *There be* structure in a real communicative context. Next, I will lead students to think about their dream room. I will show a passage about Ginny's dream room to stimulate their interest. Then, the students will share their own dream room with *There is* structure. In this way, students' thinking quality of profundity will be trained. And I can check if students can use the key words and *There is* structure correctly and confidently.

IV. Exposition

Here is my blackboard design. It presents the title of this lesson, the key words and the key sentence structures. The above blackboard design will reflect what the students have learned.

And my homework today can be divided into two kinds. Firstly, students listen to the recording 5 times to consolidate what students have learned and recite the dialogue. Secondly, students talk about their dream rooms with their classmates. It is designed to encourage students to use English to communicate with their friends.

V. Reflection

To sum up, the design of my lesson has two shining points. Firstly, I prepare the lesson from an overall perspective. Through the video of Amy's room made by myself, I lead students to visit Amy's room. Then we go to see Zhang Peng's room with Sarah and Mike. At last, I lead them to talk about their own rooms. In this way, all the activities are designed to talk about the rooms and practice *There is* structure. Secondly, students develop their autonomous learning and cooperative learning strategies through many kinds of activities. Students are asked to make predictions before listening. And students are encouraged to observe Amy's, Zhang Peng's and their own bedrooms and share their ideas with classmates. After that, they find out the similarities and differences between the rooms. Then I lead them to have a deeper thinking of their dream rooms. So their thinking quality is trained.

That's all for my lesson plan presentation. Thank you for your attention.

（说课稿撰写者：温州市沁园小学　周培培）

附：教学设计

一、 教学背景

1. 教材分析

本课是人教版《英语》五年级上册第 5 单元 There is a Big Bed 第 1 课时,是一节围绕家居陈设及其位置,即 My Room 这一话题的对话课。本课教材从 Sarah 和 Mike 参观 Zhang Peng 卧室的情景展开教学,通过书中人物对物品及物品所在地描述的对话,引导学生用 There be 句型的单数形式去描述某处的物品陈设。另外,在课文中还出现了陈述句型... is here on the ... 对物品的所在地展开描述。除此之外,教材编者在文中还渗透了评价人物和事物的表达,引导学生进行紧扣主题的语言交流。

2. 学情分析

五年级的学生通过两年的英语学习,已具备一定的英语语言能力,掌握了基本的学习方法,形成了良好的语言习惯。在此之前,学生已在 PEP 小学英语三年级下册第 4 单元中学习了物品和位置的表达方法,能够用 It's on/in/under/near the ... 句型进行描述。本课是学生学习 There be 陈述句句型的第 1 课时,所涉及的语法点只涵盖了单数,并未涉及复数,因此对学生而言,语言材料本身的难度并不大。

二、 教学目标

1. 语言交际目标

（1）能够在图片和教师的帮助下理解对话大意;能够理解生词 photo 和句型 there is ... 的意思并在语境中正确运用。

（2）能够在一定的语言情境中熟练运用 There be 句型的单数形式来描述某处存在某事物,并能用准确的语音、语调,按照正确的意群划分,朗读对话以及进行角色扮演。

2. 思维认知目标

（1）能够通过欣赏教师的自制视频,回答细节问题,增强理解层次的认知能力。

（2）能够通过判断正误、预测房间里的物品,提升分析判断层次的认知能力。

3. 社会文化目标

乐于用英语描述卧室内物品的位置。

三、 教学重难点

1. 教学重点

理解 There be 句型的单数形式并在情境中正确运用句型描述物品位置。

45

2. 教学难点

熟练运用 There be 句型,尤其是单数形式中 be 动词与后面单数名词前的冠词的正确使用,并能准确描述物品位置,是本课学习最大的难点。

四、教学准备

PPT、单词卡、微课视频、平板电脑(教师用)、学习单、学生房间的照片。

五、教学过程

Stage 1   Revision and lead-in (5 mins)

Activity 1:Free talk

Have a free talk.

T:Who is she? What's she like? (The teacher points to a girl,S1.)

S1:She's ____.

T:(S1's name). You look ____. (The teacher says to S1. Then, students are asked to use "You look …" to describe classmates and the teacher.)

【设计说明】 通过对同学和老师的自发性描述,学生激活关于形容词的背景图式,并用 You look … 进行描述性表达,使旧知与本节课即将学习的新知发生串联。同时,师生间良好的互动,可以营造轻松的英语学习氛围。

Activity 2:Sing a song

Sing the song "On,in,under" together.

Lyrics

On, in, under

On, on, in, in, under, under. The apple is on the table. The orange is in the basket. The banana peel is under my foot. The monkey is on the box. The fish is in the bowl.

【设计说明】 通过歌曲激活学生已有的关于物品以及方位表达的相关知识。

Activity 3:Brain-storming

Think about rooms in their home and tell what they can do in the rooms.

T:What is it?

Ss:(It's the living room.)

T:Yes. What do you often do in the living room?

S1:(I watch TV in the living room.)

S2:(I read books in the living room.)

T：Look，what's this?

Ss：（...）

【设计说明】 通过对各房间和其功能的回忆,激活学生关于房间和日常活动的已有知识,为学生在本课输出环节提供更多的语言框架和信息内容,并自然地将其引入到本课 bedroom 的话题学习。

Stage 2　Presentation and practice (20 mins)

Step 1　Let's learn

Activity 1：Watch and answer

Watch a video about Amy's room.

Narrator

What's in the room? There is a desk. It's big and brown. There is a red chair. There is a window near the desk. Walls, a door. There is a small bed. I like it. A sofa, a toy and a phone. There is a photo on the wall. Haha, it's me. I like my room.

T：What is the video about?

Ss：（Bedroom.）

T：Whose room is it?

Ss：（It's Amy's.）

【设计说明】 教师通过自制的视频,创设了真实的语境,讲述 Amy 房间内的物品及其位置摆放,促进学生整体感知语言的运用。

Activity 2：Look and say

Talk about the picture of Amy's bedroom with the structure "There is a/an ... in/on ..."

T：What's in the room? Look, there is a small bed. What else is in the room?

S1：（There is a ...）

T：Yes. You can use "There is a/an ...".

（The teacher teaches the sentence pattern "There is ...". Students practice it for three times and then the teacher checks three groups.）

T：What else is in the room? You can discuss with your partners.

Ss：（There is a/an ... on/in/near ...）

（If the students mentions "photo"，then the teacher teaches the word "photo" in time. If not，the teacher leads students to find out what it is，then practice "photo" with the spelling rules.）

Look and say

Amy's room

Look，this is Amy's room.

There is a/an _____ .

There is a/an _____ on/in/near _____ .

【设计说明】 在自制视频的引导下，学生关注文本的重点词句。当教师进行设问时，学生开始新语言的运用，使语言学习更加自然。

Activity 3：Let's chant

A．Listen to the chant

Lyrics

There is a desk. It's big and brown. There is a red chair. It's red. It's red. There is a window near the desk. A window, near the desk. There is a photo on the wall. Haha，it's me.

B．Chant together

【设计说明】 借助 chant 的形式，学生再次运用 There is a/an ... 句型进行表达，同时形成全篇意识。

Activity 4：Let's say

Share feelings of Amy's room. Then use the whole passage to describe Amy's room.

Let's say　Amy's room

Look，this is Amy's room.

There is a/an _____ .

There is a/an _____ on/in/near _____ .

Wow! Amy, your room is really _____ .

(nice/clean/super/good/wonderful/big/cool/...)

【设计说明】 学生结合自己对 Amy 房间的真实感受，输出一篇完整的文本。教师有意渗透如何进行物品位置的描述，如何对事物进行情感表达和评价，可以为学生接下来的自由对话提供语言框架。

Step 2　Let's try (P48)

Activity 1：Listen and tick

Firstly look at the picture (computer or TV)，then listen to the recording and check it out.

T：Zhang Peng has a room，too. Who are in the room，too?

Ss：Sarah and Mike.

T：OK. Now let's listen to the recording and try to tick the right answer：What's in Zhang Peng's room?

☐ computer ☐ TV

【设计说明】 教师借助 Let's try 的听力进入课文情境，通过前面 Amy's room 的铺垫，学生可以较轻松地做出选择。同时，利用 Let's try 的线索，教师引导学生进一步预测 Zhang Peng 房间里还有什么，使得整体情境更加流畅自然。

Step 3 Let's talk (P48)

Activity 1：Listen and choose

Firstly predict the other things in Zhang Peng's room freely，and then listen to *Let's talk*，choose the things，and check it out.

Listen and choose

There is a/an _____.

( ) ( ) ( ) ( ) ( ) ( )

【设计说明】 通过听力预测，帮助学生养成良好的听力习惯，同时培养学生推理和判断的能力。第一遍泛听促使学生整体感知语篇和语境。学生可以在根据课文录音选出房间内的物品后，丰富脑海中的文本形象。

Activity 2：Watch and answer

Answer three questions according to the video：

① What's the bed like?

② What's the photo like?

③ Where is the computer?

【设计说明】 第二遍观看促使学生再次感知文本，并深入到细节，回答相关的问题。视频的呈现方式更有利于加深学生对课文的理解和运用。

Activity 3：Read and act

A. Listen to the dialogue and mark the

Let's read

Sarah: Your room is really nice.

Zhang Peng: Thanks.

Mike: There is a big bed.

Zhang Peng: Yes. I like my bed.

Mike: There is a nice photo, too.

Sarah: Wow! You look cool!

Zhang Peng: Thank you. Hey, my computer is here on the desk. Let's play.

Tips:
升调
降调
重读

tone，stress and liaisons.

B. Read after the recording and practice reading.

C. Act out the dialogue in groups of three.

【设计说明】 在课文朗读模仿时，教师强调朗读的升降调以及重音，使学生把握朗读节奏。学生通过跟读、自由朗读、角色扮演等练习，落实教材的文本内容。

Stage 3 Consolidation and production (9 mins)

Activity 1：Talk about your room

A. Do pair work，discuss and make dialogues.

T：What's in your room? Let's talk with your partners. There is a sentence bank for you.

Sentence bank

Welcome to my room.　　Your room is really_____.

There is a/an … on/in/under …

You look …　　I like …　　… is here on the …

Let's play/read/watch …

B. Perform in front of the whole class.

【设计说明】 教师仅仅给予一些关键句子，提供学生思考的信息，不设任何的语言框架，让学生进行自由创编对话。这个方法有利于学生在课文的基础上进行发散思维，让学生根据自己的房间布置和摆设尽情地进行最真实的语言交流，表达最真实的情感。

Activity 2：Talk about your dream room

A：Enjoy the idea of Ginny's dream room.

T：Do you like Ginny's dream room?

Narrator

Hello! I'm Ginny. This is my dream room. The room is really nice. Look! The wall is pink. The floor is pink，too. There is a strawberry bed in the room. It's red. There is a watermelon sofa on the floor. It's green and red. Wow，how nice!

B：Share their dream room in groups of four.

C：Show their dream room in front of the whole class.

【设计说明】 教师给出 dream room 的概念，引发学生的积极思考。学生通过观察别人和自己的房间，欣赏 Ginny 的 dream room，想象自己的 dream room 到底会是怎么样的呢？教师通过这一部分的情景设立，更深层次地发展孩子的思维。同时，从对话填空到完整语篇呈现,不仅可以回顾本课的内容,而且有助于学生形成语篇意识。

六、 作业布置 （1 min）

1. Listen，repeat and recite the dialogue. （p48）
2. Talk about your dream room with your friends.

【设计说明】 学生通过作业 1 及时的听读模仿,复习巩固所学的知识;同时完成作业 2,鼓励学生在课后继续和朋友们分享自己的想法和观点,达到学以致用的目的。

七、 板书设计

【设计说明】 本课板书随着教学过程的推进逐步生成,以 My room 为话题,学生观察 Amy 的房间和 Zhang Peng 的房间,引出观察自己的房间,最后教师让学生思考自己梦想中的房间。核心句型和单词都在板书上清晰呈现,既囊括了本课的重点,又帮助学生巩固了本课教学内容。

八、 教学反思

这节课是一节对话课,教师以 My room 为题,巧妙创设语境,采用学习单、小组合作等形式,注重培养学生的观察能力和思维品质,循序渐进地培养学生的真实语用能力。纵观整节课,作出以下点评:

（一）解读教材,通过自制视频创设整体语境
这节课教师通过自制视频,引导学生整体感知 Amy 的房间,初识 There be 句型,通过歌

谣和语篇表达的形式,让学生加以运用,达到熟练掌握;然后教师引出 Zhang Peng 的房间,进入课文文本的解读,最后联系到学生自己的房间。在 room 的语境中,学生所需掌握的单词和句型都能得到反复操练和灵活运用。

(二)关注学生的学习活动,注重培养观察能力和思维品质

通过学习单和小组合作等形式,学生逐个突破难题,获得学习成就感。在这节课的末尾,教师还提出 Dream room 的想法,引发学生深度思考,并在小组中进行自由交流。这一想法的提出,进一步挖掘了 My room 这一主题的深度。

(教学设计者:温州市沁园小学　周培培)

说课案例五(复习课)

PEP 7 Unit 3 Plans around us Revision

微课

Hello,everyone. I am He Yuting from ZJNU. Today,I am honored to present my lesson plan here. The lesson is from PEP 7. It's a revision lesson of Unit 3 *Plans around us*.

Ⅰ. Analysis

The topic of this unit is about weekend plans,which aims to help students use the sentence pattern *be going to* to talk about things they intend to do and share their weekend plans with others. There are A,B,C,totally 3 sections in this unit and the activity forms in these sections are diverse which include *Let's try*,*Let's learn*,*Let's talk*,*Let's check*,*Let's wrap it up*,*Make a plan*,*Read and write*,*Story time* and so on.

My students are in Grade Six. They have learned English for several years so they have a relatively good foundation of English. Besides,they have learned this unit before. So they have known how to use the key sentence pattern "What are you going to do? I am going to ..." and they are familiar with the key words and phrases in this unit. However,they still have some difficulties in describing their own weekend plans and their micro-writing ability hasn't been trained yet.

Ⅱ. Statement

According to the above analysis,I set the following learning objectives.

1) Communicative competence: By the end of the class, students will be able to have a good master of the key words and phrases in this unit, such as *see a film*, *take a trip*, *buy a dictionary* and *go to the supermarket*, etc. And they will be able to flexibly use the sentence pattern "What are you going to do tomorrow? I am going to/I will ..." to communicate with others. And they will be able to describe and share their weekends.

2) Cognitive and thinking ability: With the help of cooperative learning communities, students can review key words, make travel plans as well as discuss with others. Furthermore, they will be able to know how to use Mind Map and Anchor Chart to clear thoughts and make a creative plan about their weekends.

3) Social-cultural awareness: Students will realize the importance of making a reasonable plan and they will learn to make a balance between being aspiring and being surefooted. Besides, they will feel the love between family members and hold a positive attitude towards life.

Well, this is a revision class, so the language focus is the training of using those key words, key phrases and sentence patterns in practical situations. Students may have difficulty in describing their own weekend plans clearly but their ability of raising questions on various plans should be improved. Thus, scaffolding will be provided to help them. PPT, word cards and worksheets will function as our teaching aids to facilitate the whole learning process.

III. Description

Now I will show you my teaching procedure. There are three stages, Pre-task, While-task, and Post-task. There are four activities in the first stage. In Activity 1, I will ask students to talk about their weekend plans freely by using the sentence pattern "What are you going to do? I am going to ...".

In Activity 2, an English song written by myself will be played which incorporates the key sentence patterns in this unit — *will* and *be going to*. It can not only arouse learners' interest but also create a situation for the following study. Meanwhile, students will be asked to find out the answer of this question — "What are they going to do this weekend?" while listening. In this way, their information searching ability can also be trained. In Activity 3, a worksheet will be delivered to students and they will be required to group the words on the sheet and check their pronunciations with their group members. This activity is efficient for them to go over the key words and phrases and their ability of knowledge induction can also be improved. Next, I'll check the answers with the students and ask them to read these words on the PPT together.

The second stage is While-task activities. There are five steps.

The first step is talking about your plan. It's pair work. Students will work in pairs to make a dialogue about what they are going to do. One student will ask, "What are you going to do this weekend?" The other will answer, "I am going to ..." Then I will ask other students in the class to answer the questions like "What is he/she going to do this weekend?" or "What are they going to do this weekend?" In this way, students can have a deep impression of the changes on personal pronouns in this sentence pattern and it also can attract students' attention and develop a good habit of listening.

The second step is talking about Wu Yifan's plan. Wu Yifan's plan will be shown by a mind map. The mind map has two empty blanks which are respectively under the two phrases *have a picnic* and *in the park*. Then, I will ask students some detailed information about his plan like "What is he going to do?" and "Where is he going?" to elicit the two critically important elements in a plan — "what" and "where". The two words rightly correspond to the two blanks so the mind map for Wu Yifan will be completed, which lays a good foundation for the study of the next plan.

The third step is talking about Mum's plan. There are five activities. Activity 1 is "Listen and tick". In this part, the plan of Wu Yifan's mother will be shown by a listening material and students will be asked to tick the right answers according to what they hear. The key sentence patterns will appear again in this material so that students can review them repeatedly and their listening skills can also be trained. Activity 2 is "Ask and answer questions". In this part, questions like "What's Mum's plan?" "What are uncle and aunt going to do for grandma?" and "When and where are they going to have a birthday party?" will be asked to consolidate the use of special interrogative pronouns in this key sentence pattern. Here is another key element of a plan — *when* will be introduced and students' information searching ability will be well practiced. Activity 3 is called "read and say". In order to let students have a better understanding of this warm and loving family, a conversation between Wu Yifan and his mother will be shown which is about preparing a birthday party for his grandmother. The dialogue is incomplete. Students will be asked to fill in the blanks first and then they will be divided into groups to read in roles. Activity 4 is also a pair work named "Let's wrap it up". Students will work in pairs to make sentences based on the word cards and the content of these cards can be classified into several categories such as link-verb be, personal pronouns, special interrogative pronouns and key sentence patterns. Previous activities have paved the way for this part, so I think it's not too difficult for them to finish this task. Well, to make the structure more clearly, I will summarize the use of different personal pronouns in the key sentence pattern and show it on the blackboard. Activity 5 is finishing a mind map of WuYifan's mother which can further clarify the key elements of a plan.

Up to now, Wu Yifan and his mother's plans are clear. So, what is his father's plan? Let's come to the fourth step — talk about Dad's plan. I'd like to arouse students' curiosity and encourage them to ask what they want to know about his father's plan. Their questions are mostly based on these key elements of a plan — what, where, when and how. In this way, students' questioning consciousness will be cultivated and their logical thinking and transferring ability will also be developed. After that an overall mind map will be shown and students will be required to finish writing a dialogue based on the mind map and role play it with their group members. In this part, a fresh man Robin will be introduced. He is the main character of the next step.

The last step is talking about Robin's plan on the Pluto. Two activities are involved. First, I will show them a video about the discovery of the Pluto to stimulate their interest and create a situation for the succeeding activities. After that, I will tell them Robin is going to visit the Pluto and show them an anchor chart of his weekend plan on the Pluto. Then, by checking their understanding of this chart, students will be asked to judge sentences about his plan as well as describe his plan logically and lucidly.

The last stage is Post-task activities which focus on making an anchor chart. After knowing Robin's plan on the Pluto, I think students must have a lot of fancy and fabulous ideas about life on an alien planet, so I'd like to ask them to make full use of creativity to design an anchor chart about their own weekend plan on the Pluto with their group members and describe it with the scaffolding provided. It can not only stimulate their interest in learning, but also provide a good way to go over what they have learnt. At the same time, their cooperative and communicative skills will also be practiced.

IV. Exposition

Now, look at the blackboard. It presents the title of this unit and the key elements of a plan is on the top half of the blackboard and the structure of the key sentence pattern changes with different personal pronouns, while be verbs are on the bottom. As we can see, the key points in this lesson are all presented. It is helpful for students to review what they have learned. And the key elements of a plan are shown in a way of mind map. It is clear and enlightening.

In the class, students have discussed and designed an anchor chart about their weekend plan on the Pluto, but owing to the limited time, some interesting ideas may haven't been expressed, so the homework of this lesson is to write their own weekend plan on the Pluto and share their anchor chart with their classmates. In this way, their micro-writing ability can be trained and the comprehensive language competence can also be improved.

V．Reflection

All things considered，I think there are three shining points in my lesson. First, music，video and dialogues are provided to create a situation for students，which can effectively stimulate their feelings and learning interest. Second，the cooperative leaning communities are established for students to rise above puzzles together，which are helpful for them to develop cooperative learning ability. Third，with the help of Mind Map and Anchor Chart，students' thinking ability will be practiced and they will learn how to make a reasonable plan quickly. Well，through so much practice，I am sure the learning objectives will be successfully achieved in this lesson.

OK，so much for my presentation. Thank you for your listening.

（说课稿撰写者：浙江师范大学外国语学院　何钰婷）

附：教学设计

一、 教学背景

1．教材分析

本节课是人教版《英语》六年级上册第 3 单元的复习课。本单元围绕 *My Weekend Plan* 这一话题展开。单元中的 A、B、C 三个板块分别以 Let's try，Let's talk，Let's learn，Make a plan，Read and write，Let's check，Let's wrap it up，Story time 等形式展开学习，旨在使学生能利用 be going to 结构表达即将发生的事情，积极与他人交流自己的周末计划。

2．学情分析

小学六年级的学生经过几年的英语学习，已具备一定的语言积累和知识储备，掌握了一些学习方法，他们乐于参与小组合作学习。本班学生通过本单元的学习，在语境中已基本能听、说、读、写 visit，see a film 等重点词汇和短语，tomorrow，next week 等表示将来时间的时间状语，以及 What are you going to do? I'm going to ... 等句型，基本掌握 be going to 的用法，并能与他人进行交流。但由于单元整体安排，学生还不能就单元主题 My Weekend Plan 进行小语段的输出，英语微写作技能还未能得到训练。

二、教学目标

1. 语言交际目标：

（1）能在语境中，复习核心词汇、词组和句型：visit，see a film，take a trip，go to the supermarket/...，buy a dictionary/comic book/word book/postcard，this morning/...，next week/...，tonight，tomorrow，What are you going to do? I'm going to ...，并熟练运用。

（2）能在语境中描述 My Weekend Plan on the Pluto，并分享交流。

2. 思维认知目标：

（1）能够开展"学习共同体"活动，开展自主和合作复习核心词汇、制定旅行计划，乐于与他人积极交流探讨，共同进步。

（2）能正确使用思维导图和 Anchor Chart，并发挥想象力，描述在冥王星上的周末计划。

3. 社会文化目标：

能树立在活动前做好合理计划的意识，既能"脚踏实地"，又能"仰望天空"，同时体验关爱家人、快乐生活的美好情感。

三、教学重难点

1. 教学重点：

在真实情境中正确、熟练运用本单元的核心词汇、词组和句型：visit，see a film，take a trip，go to the supermarket/...，buy a dictionary/comic book/word book/postcard，this morning/...，next week/...，tonight，tomorrow，What are you going to do? I'm going to ...

2. 教学难点：

能就各种不同的计划提出相关问题；正确描述自己的周末活动计划。

四、教学准备

PPT、学习单、词卡

五、教学过程

Stage 1　Pre-task activities（8 mins）

Activity 1：Talk about our weekend plans

Free talk about the teacher's and the students' weekend plans.

T：Hello, boys and girls. Do you like weekends?

Ss：（Yes, I do.）

T：Me too. I'm going to see a film this weekend. What are you going to do?

S1：(I'm going to ...)

T：Sounds cool. What are you going to do?

S2：(I'm going to ...)

S3：(I'm going to/will ...)

Activity 2：Listen and enjoy

Listen to and enjoy the song *This Weekend*.

This Weekend

This weekend, this weekend. We'll have a lot of fun.

We'll have a lovely picnic, a lovely picnic in the sun.

We are going to buy some food. We are going to have a barbecue.

We are going to take pictures. We are going to play a game.

This weekend, this weekend. We'll have a lot of fun.

We'll have a lovely picnic, a lovely picnic in the sun.

T：What a nice song! What are they going to do this weekend?

Ss：They're going to have a picnic/buy some food/have a barbecue/take pictures/play a game.

【设计说明】 教师利用本单元的重点句型... will/be going to ...自编一首旋律动听,朗朗上口的英语歌曲,既能激发学生的学习兴趣,又为复习环节创设情境,并提供动词词组归类的依据。

Activity 3：Read and group the words

Read the following words on the worksheet. Group the words and check the answers in groups.

T：I'm sure you have many activities to do on weekends. Now please take out your worksheet and finish Task 1. Firstly, try to read by yourself and underline the words you can't read. Secondly, practice reading the words with your group members. Lastly, group the words and check the answers in groups.

Task 1. Read and group the words

a comic book an art lesson cinema fishing a dictionary supermarket a game shopping the park a big dinner swimming the piano	Steps： 1. 自读并划出你不会的单词。 2. 四人小组相互帮助,解决困难。 3. 独立完成单词归类,组内校对。

58

> **buy** some food/＿＿＿＿＿＿＿＿/＿＿＿＿＿＿＿＿＿
>
> **have** a picnic/＿＿＿＿＿＿＿/＿＿＿＿＿＿＿＿＿
>
> **play** football/＿＿＿＿＿＿＿/＿＿＿＿＿＿＿＿＿
>
> **go** ＿＿＿＿＿＿＿/＿＿＿＿＿＿＿＿＿/＿＿＿＿＿＿＿
>
> **go to** the＿＿＿＿＿/＿＿＿＿＿＿＿＿/＿＿＿＿＿＿＿
>
> **take** pictures/**wash** clothes/**see** a film/**visit** grandparents

Read the phrases on the PPT and check the answers together.

T：Wu Yifan says, "I'm going to have a picnic this weekend. What are you going to do?"

Ss：We are going to buy some food, a comic book and a dictionary.

We are going to have a picnic, an art lesson and a big dinner.

We are going to play a game, ...

We are going fishing, ...

T：Where are you going?

Ss：We are going to the cinema, the supermarket and the park.

【设计说明】 根据本单元的学习重点和《单元学习单》反馈的难点,通过第一次"学习共同体"活动,复习核心词汇,巩固认读和意思理解,培养学生的知识归纳能力。

Stage 2　While-task activities(22 mins)

Step 1　Talk about your weekend plans

Talk about the weekend plans in pairs and answer the questions according to the dialogues.

T：Now work in pairs. One of you is Wu Yifan. Please make a dialogue with your partner and talk about your weekend plan.

S1：I'm going to have a picnic in the park this weekend. What are you going to do?

S2：(I am going to/will ...)

T：What is he/she going to do this weekend?

S3：(He/She is going to ... this weekend.)

S4：(I am going to/will ...)

S5：(I am going to/will ...)

T：What are they going to do this weekend?

S6：(They're going to ...)

【设计说明】 复习本单元重点句型。教师在学生展示对话后,适当转换人称进行提问,为复习整理不同人称的特殊疑问句做好准备,并为绘制吴亦凡周末计划的思维导图埋下伏笔;同时有效吸引学生注意力,培养倾听习惯。

Step 2　Talk about Wu Yifan's plan

Activity 1：Answer the questions and finish the mind map of Wu Yifan

T：Wu Yifan has a weekend plan. What is he going to do?

Ss：He's going to have a picnic in the park.

T：Where is he going?

Ss：He's going to the park.

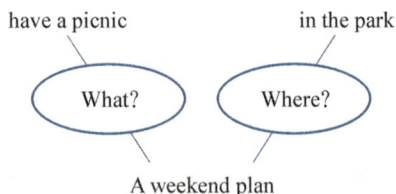

have a picnic　　　　　　　in the park

What?　　Where?

A weekend plan

【设计说明】　由吴亦凡的周末计划的活动内容和地点展开本课的第一个思维导图,从简单到复杂,为下一个计划的学习做好准备。

Step 3　Talk about Mum's plan

Activity 1：Listen and tick

Listen to the recording and finish Task 2.

T：What's Mum's plan? What are they going to do? Let's listen and tick the answers you hear.

Task II.　Listen and tick(✓)

1. It's a_____.

　　a weekend plan ☐　　a birthday party plan ☐　　a trip plan ☐

2. What are they going to do?

　　take a trip ☐　　buy some gifts ☐　　buy some flowers ☐

　　play the piano ☐　　play the guitar ☐　　make a cake ☐　　make a card ☐

【设计说明】　通过播放妈妈与吴亦凡的对话,即倾听吴妈妈为奶奶做生日派对的计划,开展听力技能训练。

Activity 2：Ask and answer questions

Answer the questions according to what you hear.

T：What's Mum's plan?

S：It's a birthday party plan.

T：What are they going to do?

Ss：They are going to have a birthday party.

T：What are uncle and aunt going to do for Grandma?

Ss：They're going to buy some gifts.

T：What is Tim going to do?

Ss：He is going to play the guitar.

T：What is Mum going to do?

Ss：She's going to make a cake.

T：What is Wu Yifan going to do?

Ss：He is going to make a birthday card.

T：When are they going to have a birthday party?

Ss：Next Saturday.

T：Where are they going to have a birthday party?

Ss：At home.

T：Where can you find the answers?

Ss：(In the first and fourth line.)

【设计说明】 就对话文本进行提问,操练本单元的重点句型,为复习以不同特殊疑问代词提问的句型做铺垫,培养学生的认读能力和信息搜索能力。

Activity 3：Read and say

Fill in the blanks. Then read aloud the whole dialogue.

T：Now，let's read the whole dialogue. Boys are Wu Yifan，and girls are Mum.

Ss：read the dialogue.

Read and say

Wu Yifan：Mum，is it Grandma's birthday next Saturday?

Mum： Yes. You're right.

Wu Yifan：What are we going to do，mum?

Mum： We're going to _____ at home.

Your uncle, aunt and cousin Tim will come.

Wu Yifan：That's nice. What are uncle and aunt going to do for Grandma?

Mum： They're going to _____.

Wu Yifan：What is Tim going to do?

Mum： He is going to _____.

Wu Yifan：Sounds cool! What are you going to do?

Mum： I'm going to _____.

Wu Yifan：Well，what am I going to do for Grandma?

Mum： I think you can _____.

Wu Yifan：Good idea! We'll have a good time.

Buy some gifts

Have a birthday party

Make a nice big cake

Make a birthday card

Play the guitar

【设计说明】 呈现对话内容,校对学习单第二个学习任务,男女学生分角色朗读对话,从字里行间体会家人之间的关爱之情。

🖥 Let's wrap it up

What are we going to do, Mum?

What are uncle and aunt going to do for Grandma?

What is Tim going to do?

What are you going to do, Mum?

What am I going to do for Grandma?

How many sentences can you make?

Activity 4：Let's wrap it up

Make the sentences with the cards in pairs. And then come to the front and make the sentences on the blackboard.

T：Look! There are some questions in the dialogue. Can you make more sentences with these words? Now take out the cards and wrap them up.

【设计说明】 提炼对话中的所有特殊疑问句做示范,帮助学生整理不同的人称及相应 be 动词在句型中的用法。

Activity 5：Finish the mind map of Mum's plan

Answer the questions and finish the mind map of Mum's plan.

T：Mum has a birthday party plan for Grandma. When is she going to have the party?

Ss：Next Saturday.

T：What is she going to do?

Ss：She's going to make a cake.

T：Where is she going to have the party?

Ss：At home.

【设计说明】 引导学生完成第二个思维导图,进一步明确制定计划需考虑时间、内容和地点,为开展了解爸爸的旅行计划的提问活动做铺垫。

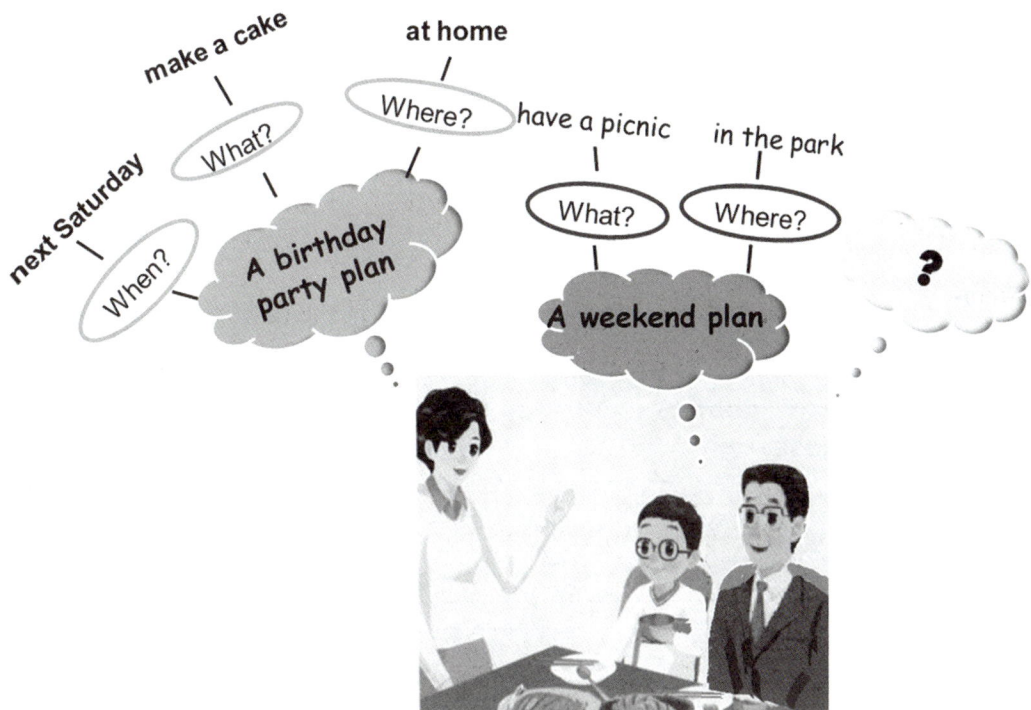

Step 4　Talk about Dad's Plan

Activity 1: Ask some questions about Dad's plan

Ask some questions about Dad's plan according to the mind map. Then check the answers with the teacher.

T: Mum has a birthday party plan. Dad has a plan, too. What is it?

Ss: A travel plan.

T: Now can you ask Dad some questions about his travel plan?

S1: (When are they going?)

T: They are going this spring festival.

S2: (Where are they going?)

T: They are going to Beijing.

S3: (How are they going?)

T: They are going by train.

S4: (What are they going to do?)

T: They're going to visit the Great Wall, Tian'anmen Square and the Bird's Nest.

　　They're going to eat roast duck and buy some paper-cut.

【设计说明】　引导学生使用特殊疑问句就爸爸的旅行计划进行提问,培养学生的问题意识,提高学生的逻辑性推理和创新迁移能力。

Activity 2: Read and role play

Complete the dialogue according to the mind map. Then act it out in groups of four.

Dad: I have a travel plan.

Wu Yifan: Really? _____?

Dad: We are going to Beijing.

Mum: _____?

Dad: This Spring Festival.

Robin: _____?

Dad: By_____.

Wu Yifan: _____?

Dad: We are going to the Great Wall. We are going to visit _____

_____.

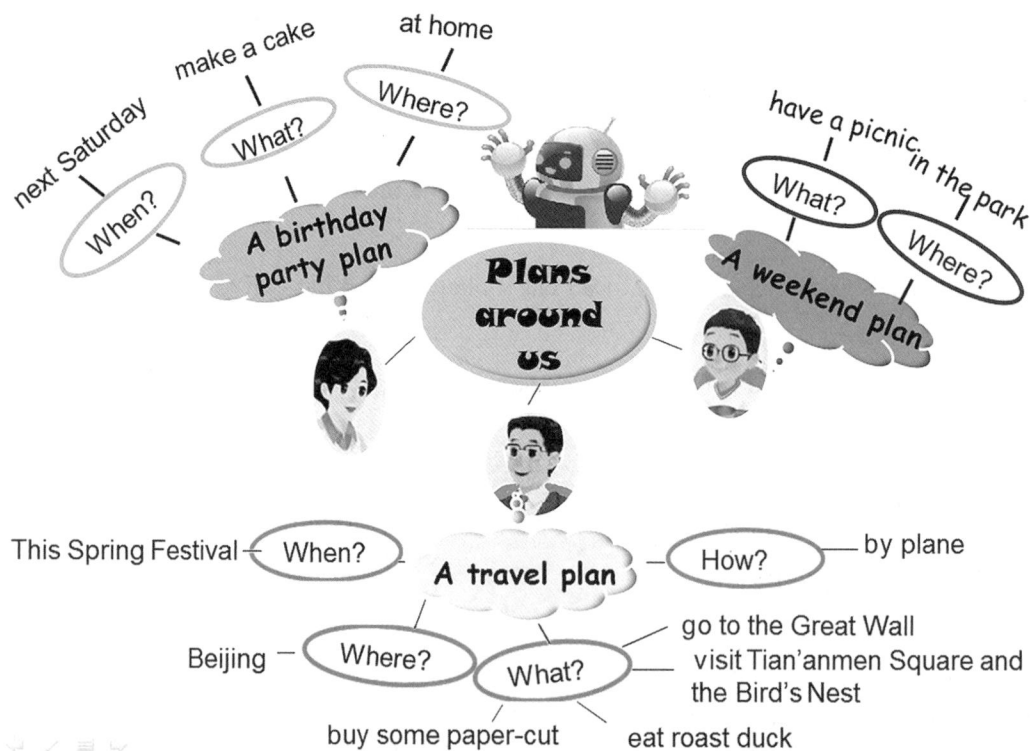

next Saturday — When?

make a cake — What? — A birthday party plan

at home — Where?

Plans around us

have a picnic — What? in the park — Where? — A weekend plan

This Spring Festival — When? — A travel plan — How? — by plane

Beijing — Where? — What? — go to the Great Wall / visit Tian'anmen Square and the Bird's Nest

buy some paper-cut — eat roast duck

【设计说明】 开展第二次"学习共同体"活动,观察爸爸旅行计划的思维导图,分角色完成对话,训练学生的知识迁移能力和逻辑思维能力。

Step 5 Talk about Robin's plan

Activity 1：Watch and read

Watch the video and read the cards.

T：Robin says he has a plan, too. What's it? Let's watch a video.

It has been over three thousand days since we left Earth. We are now almost 3 billion miles away from home. Out here where the sun is distant and faint is a place no one has ever seen before. Pluto and its system of moons, the farthest world's ever to be explored by humankind. Half a century ago we began the exploration of all the planets. Making ever more distant journeys. Each new world from Mercury to Neptune revealed its own startling complexity, character and unimagined beauty. As we now approach the Pluto system, reaching farther again. This year we are about to complete the historic era the planetary exploration. Who knows what wonders await us at these new horizons?

New Horizons

14 July, 2015

T：After about 3,000 days, 3 billion miles away from the earth, the astronomers have approached the Pluto system. They are so excited! Robin is excited, too. How about you?

Ss：（Yes, we are excited too. ）

T：Look at the cards from the Pluto. What does he say?

Ss：Dear Earthlings, thank you for not giving up on me, and thanks for visiting.

T：So Robin has a plan. He is going to visit the Pluto.

【设计说明】　播放 NASA《发现冥王星》片段,为 Robin 的周末计划创设真实情景,同时给学生打开了一个宽广的想象空间,激发他们的创作兴趣。

Activity 2：Read and judge

Read the anchor chart and judge sentences based on Robin's plan.

T：Look, Robin is very happy. He is going to visit the Pluto. He made an anchor chart about his weekend plan. Now, please read the chart and judge the sentences.

T：Robin is going to visit the robots on the Pluto on Saturday afternoon.

Ss：False. （He is going to visit the robots on the Pluto on Saturday morning. ）

T：He is going to have some Pluto burgers and ice-cream on Saturday evening.

Ss：True.

T：He is going to buy a football for Grandpa on Sunday morning.

Ss: False. (He is going to buy a gift for Grandpa on Sunday morning.)

T: He will have a busy weekend on the Pluto.

Ss: True.

Activity 3: Read and say

Read the anchor chart and describe Robin's plan clearly.

T: Now can you talk about Robin's weekend plan?

Ss: (Robin will have a busy weekend on the Pluto. On Saturday morning, he's going to visit the robots on the Pluto. In the afternoon, he is going to take some pictures of Pluto Park. In the evening, he is going to have a big dinner. On Sunday morning, he is going to buy a gift for Grandpa and send a postcard. In the afternoon, he is going to play football with his new friends. In the evening, he is going back to the earth.)

Read the anchor chart and say

My weekend plan on the Pluto

Saturday — Visit Pluto robots — Take some pictures of Pluto Park — Have a big dinner

Sunday — Buy a gift for Grandpa — send a postcard — Play football with my new friends — Go back to the earth

I'm going to visit the Pluto. Look! This is my weekend plan.

Robin will have a busy weekend on the Pluto.
On Saturday morning, he's going to... In the afternoon, ... In the evening, ...
On Sunday morning, ... In the afternoon, ... In the evening, ...

【设计说明】 将 Robin 的计划以 Anchor chart 的形式展示,将知识、逻辑、思维视觉化呈现给学生,要点更加突出,画面更加丰富,更利于学生理清思路,活学活用。教师给学生提供语言支架,展示图文表述小语段,以培养学生的综合语用能力。

Stage 3 Post-task activities(5 mins)

Activity 1: Make an anchor chart

Make new anchor charts in groups and report with the scaffolding.

We will have a . . . weekend on the Pluto. On Saturday morning, we are going to . . . In the afternoon, we . . . In the evening, . . . On Sunday morning, . . . In the afternoon, . . . In the evening, . . .

【设计说明】 第三次"学习共同体"活动,现场制作 Anchor chart,发展学生的创作性思维能力和合作能力,提高综合语用能力。

六、 作业布置

1. Write *My weekend plan on the Pluto*.
2. Share your anchor chart with your classmates.

【设计说明】 在本节课最后一个活动(小组合作现场制作 Anchor chart 并描述)的基础上,鼓励学生课后独立完成周末计划的写作,创造机会让学生分享彼此的作品,真正落实本单元微写作技能训练的教学目标,提高学生的综合语用能力。

七、 板书设计

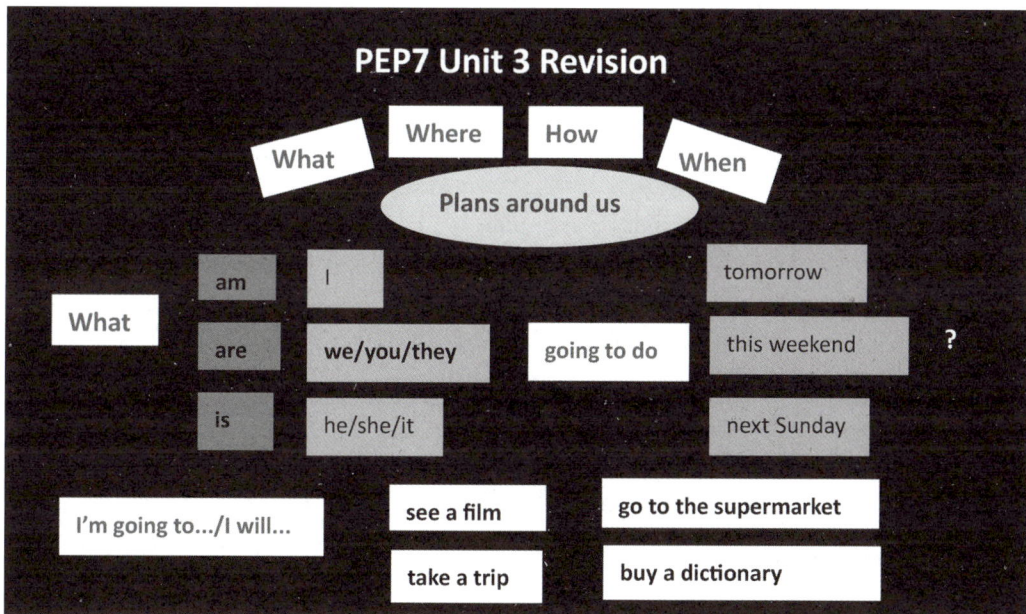

【设计说明】 本课板书随着学生活动的展开逐步生成,结构层次清晰,能够吸引学生注意力。在话题"Plans around us"周围放置四个疑问代词词卡,引导学生运用思维导图,启发思维。核心词汇、词组、句型均由学生完成摆放,既概括了本单元的重点复习内容,又调动了学生的学习积极性,教学相长。

PEP 六上 Unit 3 Revision

Plans around us

Task I. Read and group the words.

> a comic book   an art lesson   cinema
> fishing   a dictionary   supermarket
> a game   shopping   the park
> a big dinner   swimming   the piano

> Steps：
> 1. 自读并划出你不会的单词。
> 2. 在"学习共同体"中相互帮助,解决困难。
> 3. 独立完成单词归类,组内校对。

buy some food/_____/_____

have a picnic/_____/_____

play football/_____/_____

go _____/_____/_____

go to the_____/_____/_____

take pictures/**wash** clothes/**see** a film/**visit** grandparents

Task II. Listen and tick ✓

1. It's _____.

   a weekend plan ☐   a birthday party plan ☐   a trip plan ☐

2. What are they going to do?

   take a trip ☐   buy some gifts ☐   buy some flowers ☐

   play the piano ☐   play the guitar ☐   make a cake ☐   make a card ☐

Task III. Make a plan（Group work）

> **A travel plan**
>
> When? _____
> Where? _____
> How? _____
> What? _____
> _____
> _____

> Tips
> next National Day/summer holiday/...
> Harbin/Thailand/Hong Kong/London/...
> by plane/train/ship/subway/...
> go to the beach/Science Museum/Disney Land/the cinema ...
> go swimming/skiing/ice-skating/shopping/...
> buy a post card/make a snowman/eat dumplings/see the Big Ben/...

IV. Read Robin's anchor chart and judge. (√ or ×)

My weekend plan on the Pluto

Saturday — Visit Pluto robots

Take some pictures of Pluto Park

Have a big dinner

Sunday — Buy a gift for Grandpa / Send a postcard

Play football with my new friends

Go back to the earth

(　　) 1. Robin is going to visit Pluto robots on Saturday afternoon.

(　　) 2. He is going to have a Pluto burgers and ice-cream on Saturday evening.

(　　) 3. He is going to buy a football for Grandpa on Sunday morning.

(　　) 4. He will have a busy weekend on the Pluto.

V. Discuss and make your anchor chart. (Group work)

We will have a ... （happy/busy/crazy/...） weekend on the Pluto.

On Saturday morning，we're going to ...

In the afternoon，we ...

In the evening，we ...

On Sunday morning，we ...

In the afternoon，we ...

In the evening，we ...

...

(Do you like our plan? /Do you want to go with us? /Is our plan fantastic? /Is our plan interesting? /...）

八、 教学反思

本节课是单元复习课,是在单课时基础上进行的递进和延续,具有统一性、系统性和巩固性的特点。学生在《单元学习单》的指导下,主动概览知识结构,落实学习目标,开展听、说、读、写、创作等各项学习活动,综合语用能力得到了发展。

（一）自主合作学习，提高学生学习能力

通过"学习共同体"活动，学生既有独立思考又有合作互动，在课堂情境中能清晰地向同伴表达思想，听取和讨论他人的思想，并在此过程中重构自己的思想，实现主动参与、自我监控与自我调节，自觉地、主动地习得新知识，学习能力得到相应提高。

（二）使用思维导图，提升学生思维品质

学生通过本课的前置性作业和课堂中的 4 次思维导图的运用，以及其他形式的复习活动，其批判性、发散性、逻辑性、迁移性和创造性思维得到训练，思维品质进一步提升。

（三）挖掘教材内容，培养学生文化意识

根据本单元的教材文本和图片，挖掘一些可拓展内容，将本复习课的主题定为"Plans around us"。4 个计划与学生生活紧密联系，并蕴含着不同的文化内涵，但传达给学生活动前做好合理计划的意识是一致的。

（四）创设真实情境，丰富学生情感体验

学生在歌曲创设的"愉快周末"情境、对话创设的"生日派对"情境、视频创设的"太空探索"情境中，得到真实的情感体验，学习关爱家人，体会亲情的美好；同时不忘梦想，学会"仰望星空"。

（教学设计者：温州广场路小学　张碧炜）

说课案例六（对话课）

PEP 5 Unit 6 In a nature park Part A Let's talk

Hello，everyone! I'm Jiang Manman from Oujiang Primary School. It's my great honor to present my lesson plan here.

微课

Ⅰ. Analysis

The lesson I'll present is Unit 6 *In a nature park* Part A Let's talk，PEP 5. The lesson type is listening and speaking. The topic of this lesson is "nature park". The purpose of this lesson is to let students learn the key words *nature park*，*river*，*lake*，*forest* and to use the question-form of *There be* structure "Is there ...? — Yes, there is. / No，there isn't." as well as the structure *Let's go+doing* to describe what people can do in a place.

My students are in Grade 5 of primary school. They have obtained basic language knowledge and learning strategies. They are happy to work in groups and learn cooperatively. What's more, they have learned *There be* structure in Unit 5, which is a good preparation for this lesson. Therefore, the learning difficulties will be greatly reduced.

II. Statement

After analyzing the teaching material and the learners, the learning objectives will be presented as follows.

As for communicative competence, firstly, students will be able to understand the general idea of the dialogue, grasp useful words and expressions such as *nature park*, *river*, *lake*, *forest*, and they will be able to use the sentence pattern "Is there ...? — Yes, there is. /No, there isn't. " correctly in real communicative contexts. Secondly, students can read the dialogue aloud with correct pronunciation, intonation, stress, and act it out.

As for cognitive and thinking ability, firstly, students will be able to improve their analyzing and applying abilities by elaborating and making comments on the nature parks designed by themselves. Secondly, students will be able to deepen their understanding of the text and improve the language understanding ability by role play and imitation.

As for social-cultural awareness, students' love for the beautiful parks will be evoked and they will give suggestions to protect the polluted parks as well.

The language focus of this lesson is to let students understand and use the question-form of *There be* structure in different contexts. The pronunciation of the sentence "Is there ...?" is the difficult point in this lesson.

III. Description

Along with the analysis and statement of my lesson plan, here comes the teaching procedure. It can be divided into four stages: warming up, pre-task, while-task and post-task.

The first stage is warming up. There are two steps at this stage. In the first step, students will sing a song *In the classroom*, which can motivate their interest and lead them into English learning as quickly as possible. At the same time, students will practice *There be* structure they've learned. In the second step, students will review the words quickly by matching adjectives and nouns to create different phrases with the light background music. Students can pronounce the words quickly without dragging.

Based on the warming up, pre-task is designed as the second stage, which consists of three steps. In Step One, students will learn the pattern: Is there ...? — Yes, there is. / No, there isn't. I will present an empty basket and things for a picnic and ask students to guess what is in the basket by using the sentence pattern "Is there ...?". Students will guess the answer "Yes, there is. /No, there isn't." (If yes, the things will fly to the basket; if no, the things will disappear.) Then students will work in pairs to guess the things in the basket. With the help of PPT dynamic effect, the word "is" will be taken out and put at the very beginning of the sentence, through which students can learn the sentence pattern easily. In Step Two, I will elicit the title "Nature park". Firstly, the basket flies to a nature park with a rhyme and I will ask students to guess where the basket is. Then students will chant aloud to practice *Let's go+doing* structure, which will make a good preparation for the following learning. In Step Three, students will learn the dialogue among Miss White and the children, which talks about the nature park they are going on the school outing day. Students will watch the video without subtitles. They will try to understand the general idea and answer the question "Which nature park are they going to?" Then, students will listen again, fill in the blanks and learn the words *river*, *lake* as well.

After talking about what there are in the nature park, here comes the third stage, while-task. I will design two steps. In Step One, students will listen to the dialogue on Page 58 "Let's try" part and answer the question "What's in the park?" in order to elicit the new word *forest*, and students will know that there is a forest in the Green Nature Park. In Step Two, students will learn the dialogue in the textbook. Firstly, students will listen to the dialogue and answer the question "What's in the forest?" Through the first listening, students will perceive the whole text. Secondly, students will watch the video and answer the question "What does Zhang Peng want to do?" Next, students will listen to the dialogue and repeat it sentence by sentence. It aims to instruct students to use the right pronunciation and intonation when they read aloud. Then, students will try to make up a dialogue with blackboard notes. Lastly, students will do a role play in groups and act it out.

The fourth stage is post-task. At this stage, there are two steps. In the first step, I will show the nature park designed by Mike as an example to arouse their love for the beautiful parks. In the second step, firstly I will show some nature parks, some of which are beautiful, while some are a little dirty. Then students will design a nature park in groups and try to describe it with the sentence pattern: There is/are ... in the nature park. After that, students will guess what's in the nature park with other groups by using the pattern: Is there ...? — Yes, there is. /No, there isn't. Finally, group leaders will describe the nature parks they designed and give suggestions to protect the polluted parks. Emotion education is filled in every section of teaching. In this part, I'll try to encourage all the students to participate in the talk with the language learned.

IV. Exposition

Here is my blackboard design. On the left are some key words and sentences. They will lead students to focus on these language points and also offer some hints when they describe their parks. On the right are the parks students designed. When they observe the beautiful parks and the polluted parks directly, students will have a deeper impression.

Finally, let's come to homework. Firstly, students will listen to the tape and act out the dialogue on Page 58. It aims to help students consolidate what they have learned in the class. Secondly, students should describe their nature parks to their partners after class, which is designed to encourage students to use language they've learned to communicate with others.

V. Reflection

To sum up, my lesson has the following shining points：

First, based on the learners, I restructure the text. In my design, I don't only adhere to the textbook but restructure the text, using pictures, rhymes, songs and so on to create different situations.

Second, with emotion education, I cultivate students' good behaviors. The students need a class to experience beauties in life. So in this lesson, students will compare the beautiful parks with the polluted parks. Through it they will develop their awareness of environmental protection and give suggestions to the polluted parks.

That's all for my presentation. Thanks for your attention.

（说课稿撰写者：温州市鹿城区瓯江小学　蒋曼曼；宁波江北区外国语艺术学校　马米雪）

附：教学设计

一、教学背景

1. 教材分析

本课是一节对话课,内容选自人教版 PEP 小学英语五年级上册第 6 单元 *In a nature park* 中的 A 部分 Let's talk。教材文本通过对话的形式,让学生用一般疑问句的问答句型 (Is there ...? — Yes, there is. /No, there isn't.)讨论公园里有什么;同时,要求学生认读并运用文中出现的词汇,如 nature park, river, lake, forest 等。另外,教材编者在文末加入了 Let's ... 句型,融入了在某一地点的人物活动,丰富了语言交流。

2. 学情分析

五年级的学生经过两年的英语学习,已经具备了一定的语言基础和知识储备,掌握了一些学习方法。他们乐于参与小组合作学习。就本课而言,学生在第5单元的话题 Room 中已经学习了 There be 句型的陈述句形式,了解了相应的单复数形式变化,为本课的疑问句教学做好了铺垫,并在此基础上建构新的知识。

二、 教学目标

1. 语言交际目标:

(1) 能够在图片和教师的帮助下理解对话大意,在具体的语境中理解与运用词汇:nature park, river, lake, forest 和句型:Is there ... ? Yes, there is. /No, there isn't.

(2) 能够按照正确的语音、语调及意群朗读对话,并能进行角色扮演。

2. 思维认知目标:

能通过听力、对话、同伴互助合作等学习方式完成相关教学任务,促进自主学习,提高思维能力和口语交际能力。

3. 社会文化目标:

通过对自然公园的设计,感受公园的美丽,并对受污染的公园提出治理建议。

三、 教学重难点

1. 教学重点:

能在语境中理解并运用"Is there ... ? Yes, there is. /No, there isn't"等句型进行简单问答。

2. 教学难点:

能正确读出 Is there ... 句型的发音。

四、 教学准备

多媒体课件、课堂导学小帮手、单词卡、录音机、教学视频、头饰和学生活动设计的材料。

五、 教学过程

Stage 1 Warming-up (2 mins)
Step 1 Sing a song
Sing a song *In the classroom* together.

```
Lyrics
                          In the classroom

In the classroom，in the classroom，

there's a blackboard on the wall.

There are pictures，there are flowers，

In the classroom，where we learn.
```

【设计说明】 歌曲激趣,使学生尽快进入英语学习状态,并操练已学的 There be 句型。

Step 2　Review the words

Match adjectives and nouns quickly and create different phrases.

	Can you read?	
a butterfly a zoo A bench A boat A bird		white, green, blue, clean, polluted, wonderful, quiet, beautiful, super, great, cool, nice …

【设计说明】 快速激活已学单词记忆,配以轻松快速的背景音乐,使学生养成发音干脆、不拖音的好习惯,同时也为之后的文本输出做好铺垫。

Stage 2　Pre-task (6 mins)

Step 1　Learn the pattern：Is there …? Yes, there is. /No, there isn't.

The teacher presents an empty basket as well as things for a picnic（see PPT）. Students guess the things in it and do pair work.

Activity 1：Guess "What is in the basket?", using the pattern "Is there …?".

Activity 2：Guess the answer：Yes，there is. /No，there isn't. （If yes，the things will fly to the basket；if no，the things will disappear. ）

Activity 3：Do a pair work and talk about the things given.

S1：Is there a kite?

S2：Yes，there is.

S1：Is there a football?

S2：No，there isn't.

【设计说明】 通过猜测 What's in the basket? 在一定的信息沟设置中,从已学陈述句 There is … 自然地过渡到新授的疑问句 Is there …? 利用 PPT 动态效果呈现,把 is 提前,让学生更直观感受新授句型的构成,加深学生的记忆,降低学习难度。

Step 2　Elicit the title：Nature park

Activity 1：Listen to a rhyme

Guess where the basket is（in the nature park）and listen to a rhyme about nature park.

> The grass is green. The sky is blue. The air is clean. The day is new. The wind blows. The clouds play. The river flows. Beautiful day，beautiful day.

【设计说明】　通过一幅自然公园的美景和一首活泼轻快的 rhyme，引出本课课题 Nature park。

Activity 2：Chant

Chant aloud to practice *Let's go+doing* structure.

> Go to the nature park. Let's go fishing. Nice! Nice!
> Go to the nature park. Let's go hiking. Super! Super!
> Go to the nature park. Let's go boating. Cool! Cool!

【设计说明】　朗朗上口的 Chant 将句型和形容词巧妙地结合在一起，既活跃了课堂气氛，又操练了句型，为之后教授文本对话做铺垫。

Step 3　Learn the dialogue among Miss White ＆ Children

Activity 1：Understand the whole text

Teacher presents the dialogue among Miss White and the children. Students watch the flash with sound one by one without subtitles. Students understand the general idea and answer the question："Which nature park are they going to?"

> **Let's watch**
>
> Miss White and the kids are talking in the classroom.
>
> Chen Jie：Is there a swing in the Green Nature Park? I want to play with it.
>
> Miss White：No，there isn't.
>
> Mike：Is there a slide in the Green Nature Park? I want to play with it.
>
> Miss White：No，there isn't.
>
> Zhang Peng：Is there a river in the Green Nature Park? I want to go fishing.
>
> Miss White：No，there isn't.

【设计说明】　再构文本，通过引入 Miss White 和学生在教室的讨论，将学生置于一定的语境中整体感知对话文本。学生从听到的文本中提取有效信息进行问答。

Activity 2：Learn two words：river,lake

Listen again and fill in the blanks and learn the words *river*，*lake*.

【设计说明】 再听文本,引出所授词汇 river 和 lake,训练学生听力能力并促进学生对文本内容的理解。

Stage 3　While-task（15 mins）

Step 1　Let's try

Listen to the dialogue on page 58 and answer the question，"What's in the park?" then learn the new word "forest".

【设计说明】 通过 Let's try 部分引出新授单词 forest。

Step 2　Let's talk

Activity 1：Listen and answer

Listen to the tape and answer the question，"What's in the forest?"

【设计说明】 回归课文,通过听对话让学生整体感知文本。

Activity 2：Watch and answer

Watch the video and answer the question，"What does Zhang Peng want to do?"

【设计说明】 带着问题看视频,加深学生对文本的理解。通过回答,逐一呈现文本内容并模仿跟读,降低了学生学习难度。

Activity 3：Repeat and imitation

Listen to the dialogue and repeat it sentence by sentence with reading skills, such as stress, intonation and so on.

【设计说明】 指导学生用正确的语音语调进行角色朗读,培养学生朗读技巧。

Activity 4：Make up a dialogue

Make up a dialogue with the help of blackboard notes.

【设计说明】 让学生观察、思考、理解、记忆和消化教学内容的过程。

Activity 5：Role play

Do a role play in groups and act the dialogue out.

【设计说明】 在扮演过程中,教师让学生戴好事先准备好的头饰,让学生有真实的角色体验,置身于文本情境中。

Stage 4　Post-task（12 mins）

Step 1　Watch and answer

Watch the video about the nature park designed by Mike and answer the question，"Do you like Mike's park?"

【设计说明】 通过 Mike 设计的公园和他的描述,学生巩固句型的同时,激发了对美丽公园

Group work

Step1: Design a nature park with your partner.
（贴一贴，和你的同伴设计一个自然公园。请用 "There is...in the nature park" 句型进行表述。）
Step2: Guess what's in the nature park with other groups.
（猜测其他组所设计的自然公园里有什么。请用 "Is there ...?" 句型进行交流。）
Step3: Describe the nature park you designed.
(向大家描述你们组所设计的自然公园。)

cloud lake river forest elephant monkey

fountain

flower

grass

ZOO

的喜爱之情，情感得到了升华。

Step 2   Talk about your nature park

Teacher shows some nature parks. Some are beautiful, while others are a little dirty.

Activity 1：Design and say

Design a nature park in groups and try to say with the structure *There is ... in the nature park*.

【设计说明】 学生小组合作设计自己的自然公园。在拼拼贴贴的过程中，启发思维，运用句型 *There is ... in the nature park*，在同伴交流互助的过程中学会用英语进行交谈。

Activity 2：Guess and describe

Guess what's in the nature park with other groups, using the pattern *Is there ...? Yes, there is. / No, there isn't*. Then the group leaders describe the nature parks they designed and give suggestions to protect the dirty parks.

【设计说明】 通过交流，学生发现有 beautiful parks 和 dirty parks 两类公园。让学生综合运用本课所学的句型，对受污染的公园提出建议，力求引导学生的全员参与，践行以生为本的教学理念。

Activity 3：Summarize

Among the parks students designed, they get to know that we have beautiful parks. They are clean. But in our daily life, there are many polluted parks. They are dirty.

【设计说明】 在充分感受本文中公园之美后,通过交流,使学生发现在现实生活中还有很多受污染的公园。情感教育渗透在每一步的教学环节中,至此水到渠成。无痕的德育渗透,升华了主题。

六、 作业布置

1. Act out the dialogue on page 58.

2. Describe your nature park after class and talk about it with your partners.

【设计说明】 角色扮演、朗读对话有助于复习巩固新单词与句型。向同伴描述自己设计的公园这一任务旨在鼓励学生运用所学新知识,进行交流。

七、 板书设计

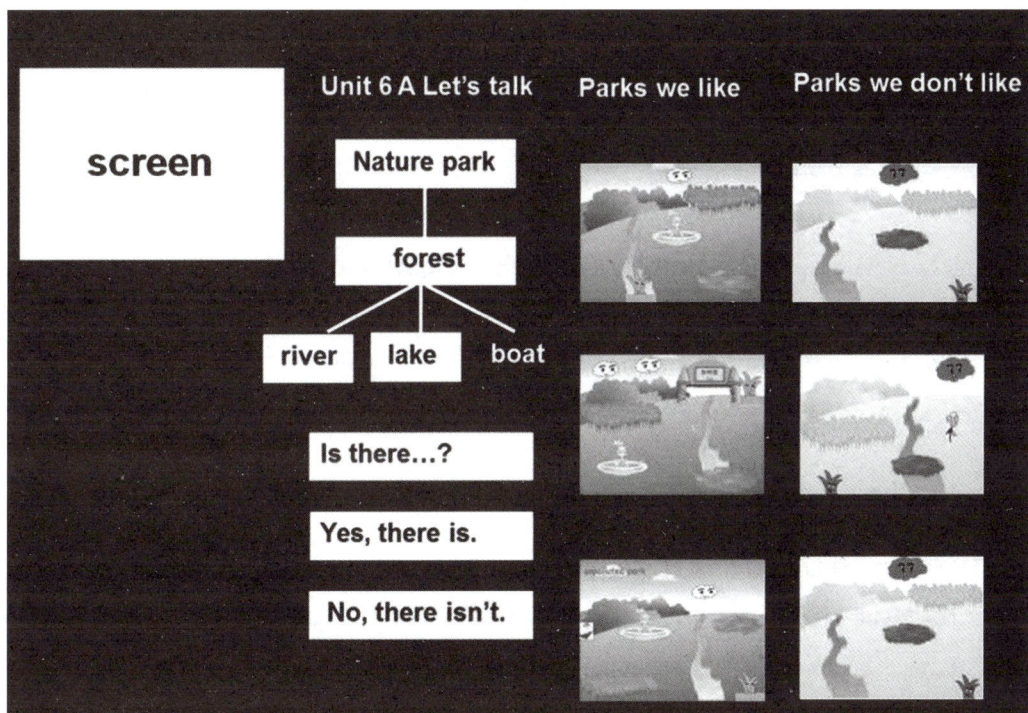

【设计说明】 重点单词与句型的呈现能让学生引起重视,加深记忆。学生在描述自己设计的公园时也有所参考。此外,教师会在黑板上粘贴学生设计的公园并进行分类,学生直观地感受到无污染公园和受污染公园的差别,激发他们保护环境的意识。

八、 教学反思

反思本节课,我得到了以下思考和启发:

（一）基于学情，再构文本

在本堂课的教学设计中，我根据学生的实际情况和语境的真实性，运用图片、童谣、歌曲等形式，对 Miss White 和 Children 在教室里讨论 school outing day 将要去自然公园一事会产生怎样的对话进行文本再构，力求以语篇对话带动词与句型的学习，以符合学情的语量输入，优化学生的语言输出。

（二）品行培养，追求美好

本堂课注重育人教育。学生需要一个有感悟的课堂来体会生活中的美好。通过受污染的公园和无污染公园的对比，学生能用英语表达对公园美的喜爱，并对受污染公园提出一些治理措施和建议。在文本的推进中学生感悟到我们要保护公园，在巩固所授内容的同时得到了情感的升华。

（教学设计者：温州市鹿城区瓯江小学　蒋曼曼）

说课案例七（读写课）

PEP 5 Unit 2 My week B Read and write

Good morning, everyone! I'm Cathy. It's my great honor to present my lesson plan here. The lesson I will present is from PEP 5 Unit 2 *My week* B *Read and write*.

微课

Ⅰ. Analysis

The topic of this lesson is week schedules. The teaching material can be divided into three parts. The first part focuses on Wu Yifan's week schedule, the second is about Robin's advice on Wu Yifan's schedule and the third is the writing part. The teaching materials are designed to help students read through scanning, skimming and picture, and using key words and sentences to complete the writing in the third part.

My students are in Grade 5. They are primary school students in Zhejiang Province. They are active in class, and they also desire to perform in the front of classroom. Before this lesson, students have learned some reading skills, such as skimming and scanning. And they are able to search for information from pictures and listening materials. Students have learned to use the sentences "What do you have on ... s?", "I have ...", "I often ..." and "Do you often ...?" in the previous lessons. But they haven't been able to use the words and key sentences in writing. In this lesson, I will focus on helping students analyze and integrate text information in the topic of week schedule and express themselves in English.

II. Statement

Based on the above analysis, I set the following learning objectives. As for communicative ability, firstly, students will be able to review the key words, such as *advice*, *tired*, and these sentences in the reading part, and complete the dialogue about Wu Yifan's new schedule in the writing part; secondly, they will use these sentence patterns to talk about their weekend schedules, and finish the writing of *My advice*; thirdly, they will be able to read the dialogue with correct pronunciation and intonation. For thinking and cognitive ability, firstly, students will develop their cognitive thinking ability of comprehension through ticking or crossing and retelling Wu Yifan's new schedule. Secondly, their cognitive thinking ability of evaluation will be well developed through evaluating the schedules of Wu Yifan and David. Thirdly, they will also be able to train their cognitive thinking ability of creation by designing their weekend schedules based on others' advice. For social-cultural awareness, students will realize the importance of moderate exercise, and they can make a reasonable week schedule.

The lesson type is reading and writing, so the language focus is helping students understand the whole passage and write a reasonable weekend schedule for themselves with the help of others' advice. But the writing task is a little difficult for them. In order to achieve the above objectives and deal with the language focus and difficulty, I will adopt PWP teaching mode to integrate reading and writing. PPT, word cards and blackboard will be used to support the whole teaching process.

III. Description

Now let's come to my teaching process. The whole lesson can be divided into three stages, pre-reading, while-reading and post-reading.

In pre-reading stage, there are two steps: warming up and free talk. In the step of warming up, there are two activities. Firstly, I will show them a video about Japanese Olympic advertising in 2016 to attract students' attention. And then, we will do a brainstorming. Students will be required to review the words about time such as *Monday*, *Wednesday*, *Sunday*, and activities they often do, such as *watch TV*, *do homework*, *read books*. In this way, students' previous knowledge can be activated. This step will lay a solid foundation for the following steps. The second step is *Free Talk*. There are also two activities. In the first activity, I will show my weekend card. Then I will lead students to talk about their weekend with sentence patterns, *What do you often do on ... /the weekend? I often ... Sometimes I ... Do you often ...? Yes, I do. No, I don't.* After that, students will work in pairs to talk about their weekend. Students will be curious about my weekend, so they will be willing to say something about their weekend. In Activity 2, I will show them their lesson schedule and ask them some questions like" *When do you have PE class? Do you often do sports after PE class?*" to consolidate what they have learnt before and lead in the topic of proper week schedules. And the new word *schedule* will be presented here.

And then comes the while-reading stage. There are three steps: Wu Yifan's schedule, Robin's advice and the writing part. Step 1 is about Wu Yifan's schedule, and there are four activities in it. In Activity 1, students will listen to the recording of the passage and then answer a question: *What does Wu Yifan have on Friday?* Next, students will be asked to guess the meaning of the word *tired* according to a picture. In this part, students can search for information from the pictures provided on the textbook. It is beneficial to their information-searching ability. In Activity 2, students will read the whole passage with the question "What do Wu Yifan and Robin talk about?" to get the general idea. Then I will let students read the first part quickly and answer the questions "Why does Wu Yifan look tired?" and "Does Wu Yifan often play sports?" to train their information-searching ability. At the same time, my students will learn the phrase *play sports* and they will realize that Wu Yifan lacks exercise. In Activity 3, students will be asked to read the passage more carefully and finish the Tick or Cross task. It aims to check students' understanding of this passage and train their cognitive thinking ability of comprehension. Students will listen to the tape twice and read after it in Activity 4. During this process, students can not only check their pronunciation and intonation but also look through the passage again and circle what they haven't understood. Step 2 is about Robin's advice. Firstly, we will talk about the new schedule in Activity 1, which is given by Robin. And the words *should*, *advice* and *every day* will be presented in his advice. Then I will analyze this schedule step by step so that students will know the importance of doing sports. In Activity 2, students will be asked to retell the new schedule with the given structure. This activity can train students' abilities of language organization and information integration and lay a foundation for the writing part. Step 3 is the writing part, students will finish writing the dialogue about the new schedule. I will show students how to write in one-line lattice carefully and give them some tips to finish the dialogue. Students will pay attention to the writing standard and I can check their understanding of this passage again.

The last stage is post-reading. There are two steps: David's schedule and students' weekend schedule. In the first step, I will introduce another boy David to them. He is active. He plays basketball every day. First, I will let students talk about their opinions about this schedule. Then I will guide them to understand that doing sports is good for our health, but excessive sports or being indulged in doing sports may be harmful. Thus, they will be aware that they should keep a balance in doing sports, and it also trains their cognitive thinking ability of evaluation. Then in the next step, students will be asked to work in pairs to make appropriate weekend schedules for themselves through others' advice and show it in front of the class. It aims to consolidate the use of the sentence patterns they have learned and train their cognitive thinking ability of creation. These activities will not only help students develop cooperation ability, but also cultivate their awareness of doing moderate sports to keep healthy.

IV. Exposition

Now, let's see the blackboard design. It presents the title of this lesson on the top of the blackboard. The key sentence patterns in this unit are put on the left part. The key words are shown on the right half. In this way, students can clearly know the key points in this lesson and they can also have a deep impression of what they have learnt. It also helps students participate in the lesson activities. And there is also a competition corner to activate students' motivation of English learning.

How to help students make an appropriate schedule is a difficult point of this lesson, so I'd like to ask them to finish writing *My advice* after class and share it with their deskmates. This is the first homework. The second homework is to read this passage aloud for about 10 – 15 minutes, because there is less attention in English speaking in this lesson. It will train students' pronunciation and intonation.

V. Reflection

Generally speaking, my lesson has three shining points. Firstly, in my lesson, the basic reading skills such as skimming, scanning and writing skills are both trained. Secondly, students' thinking qualities are improved. Their cognitive thinking ability of comprehension, evaluation and creation will be well developed through the activities such as Tick or Cross, retelling, evaluating the schedules of Wu Yifan and David, and designing a reasonable schedule based on suggestions from others. At last, by sharing the idea that moderate exercise is beneficial to our health, students will develop a scientific concept of doing sports.

That's all for my presentation. Thank you for your attention.

（说课稿撰写者：浙江师范大学外国语学院　范淑丹）

附：教学设计

一、教学背景

1. 教材分析

本节课为读写课，内容选自人教版《英语》五年级上册第二单元 *My week* 中的 B 读写部分。本单元的话题为周计划，重点句型有 What do you have on . . . s? I have . . . . Do you often . . .？I often . . . . 等。本课的教材可以分为三部分：第一部分为 Wu Yifan's schedule，呈现了 Wu Yifan 和 Robin 关于 Wu Yifan 日常活动的对话，可以从中看出他不喜欢运动；第二部分是 Robin's advice，Robin 建议 Wu Yifan 加强锻炼，并为他制定了新的运动时间表；第三部分是 Writing part，让学生根据新的时间表，补齐 Wu Yifan 和 Sarah 的对话。教材旨在辅助学生运用速读、扫读和结合图片理解文本信息等阅读技能完成阅读，并运用相关单词和句型完成第三部分的写作。

2. 学情分析

本课教学对象是小学五年级学生，他们生性活泼好动，具有较强的好奇心和表现欲。经过两年多的英语学习，学生们已经掌握了基础的学习方法和一些阅读技巧，如扫读和跳读，并能从图片和听力材料中搜索到所需的信息。学生们已经在本单元之前的学习中学会使用 What do you have on . . .？I have . . . Do you often . . .？I often . . . 等句型进行对话，但学生们还不具备运用本课单词和重点句型完成写作的能力。

二、教学目标

1. 语言交际目标

（1）能够在阅读中巩固本单元新词和句型如 advice，tired，What do you have on . . .？并将其用于第三部分补齐 Wu Yifan 和 Sarah 的对话。

（2）能够按照正确的语音、语调及意群朗读对话。

（3）能够运用 I have . . . on . . . I often . . . 等句型谈论自己的周末计划，并完成作文 My advice。

2. 思维认知目标

（1）能够通过判断对错、复述时间表等活动，培养理解层次的认知能力。

（2）能够通过评价 Wu Yifan 和 David 的时间表，培养评价层次的认知能力。

（3）能够根据对 Wu Yifan 和 David 的建议，设计合理的时间表，培养创造层次的认知能力。

3. 社会文化目标

能够合理地制定自己的周计划，并意识到运动的重要性，养成勤做运动的习惯。

三、 教学重难点

1. 教学重点

熟练运用扫读和略读的阅读技巧，并学会借助图片内容帮助自己理解文本，运用已学单词和句型完成第三部分的写作，并根据他人建议为自己制定合理的周计划。

2. 教学难点

利用所学的词汇和句子完成第三部分的写作，并根据他人的建议为自己制定合理的周计划。

3. 教学准备

多媒体、PPT、单词卡片、黑板。

四、 教学过程

Stage 1   Pre-reading (8 mins)

Step 1   Warming up (3 mins)

Activity 1：Watch a video

Enjoy a video about Japanese Olympic advertising in 2016.

【设计说明】 教师采用了视听教学法，展现视频片段，吸引学生的注意力。

Activity 2：Brainstorm

Have a brainstorming about weekdays and activities they do.

T：Monday.

S1：Play football.

T：Tuesday.

S2：Play basketball.

...

【设计说明】 活跃班级气氛，激活学生已有的知识储备，复习关于 weekdays 的名词和其他动词短语。

Step 2   Free talk (5 mins)

Activity 1：Talk about the weekend

Talk about the weekend with their classmates using adverbs such as *often* and *sometimes*.

T：Look！This is my weekend. On the weekend，I ... What about your weekend?

S1：（On the weekend，I often play ping-pong. Sometimes I watch TV. ）

T：Let's work in pairs and talk about your weekend with your partner.

S1：（What do you often do on the weekend?）

S2：（I often play football. Sometimes I watch TV. ）

S1：（Do you often read books?）

S2：（Yes，I do. ）

【设计说明】 教师结合自身实际的周末运动计划,导入本课话题周计划,同时激发了学生的好奇心,让学生有话可讲,也锻炼了学生的语言组织能力。此外,本活动的句型操练可以为下一个活动谈论周计划做铺垫。

Activity 2：Talk about schedules

Have a free talk about the lesson schedule with the teacher.

T：When do you have PE class? （Shows the lesson schedule on the PPT）

S1：（I have PE class on Tuesdays and Fridays. ）

T：This is a schedule of our class. （Students practice the word "schedule". ）

T：How many PE lessons do you have every week? Is it too many or too few?

S1：（We have two PE lessons. I think it's too few. ）

T：Why?

S1：（Because I like PE very much. ）

S2：（I think it's too many. I don't like PE. ）

T：Do you often do sports after PE class?

S1：（Yes，I do. ）

S2：（No，I don't. ）

...

【设计说明】 通过课程表的呈现,引导学生利用已学句型谈论自己平时的周计划,并反思一周的运动量,导入合理运动的话题。

Stage 2　While-reading (20 mins)

Step 1　Wu Yifan's schedule (8 mins)

Activity 1：Listen and answer

Listen to the tape of the whole passage and answer the questions.

T：This is Wu Yifan's schedule. Now，let's listen and answer. What does Wu Yifan have on Fridays?

S：（He has a PE lesson. ）

T：Wu Yifan has PE. Look at this picture. Wu Yifan lies on the sofa after PE class.

Look and answer：How does Wu Yifan feel?

A：He is happy.   B：He is tired.

A：高兴的   B：疲倦的

【设计说明】 学生听完录音并回答问题,接着通过图片猜测单词 tired 的词义。在这一活动中,学生通过听力和图片搜索,阅读信息的技能得到了训练,且学生在此过程中逐渐接触到本课的话题——“运动”。

Activity 2：Fast reading

Read the passage and choose the answers.

T：Read the whole passage and tell me what Wu Yifan and Robin are talking about.

S1：(C. PE and weekend.)

T：How do you know that?

S1：(I have PE. /What do you often do on the weekend?)

T：Please read the first part quickly and tell me why Wu Yifan looks tired. Does Wu Yifan often play sports?

S1：(A. He has PE.)

T：Why?

S1：(I have PE.)

S2：(B. No，he doesn't.)

T：Why?

S2：(No，I don't. I don't like sports.)

【设计说明】 通过扫读、跳读和选择题的辅助,学生可以迅速把握课文的大意。阅读对话第一部分并回答问题可以锻炼学生快速搜寻关键信息的阅读技能。

Activity 3：Careful reading

Read the passage carefully and tick or cross，and then check the answer together. (Tip：circle key words or sentences.)

Read carefully

Robin：You look tired. What do you have on Fridays?

Wu Yifan：I have PE.

Robin：Do you often play sports?

Wu Yifan：No，I don't. I don't like sports.

Robin：What do you often do on the weekend?

Wu Yifan：I often watch TV. Sometimes I read books.

【设计说明】 Tick or cross 活动原本属于第二部分,为及时检测学生对第一部分文本的理解,因而把 Tick or cross 活动提前。学生需仔细阅读整篇文章,找出细节信息。该活动有助于训练学生的信息查找能力,同时引导学生根据文本中的依据改正表达,既可以锻炼学生的分析对比能力,又可以培养学生理解层次的思维能力。

Activity 4：Listen and imitate

Listen to the tape and repeat. Pay attention to the pronunciations and intonations. While reading, circle the words or sentences they don't understand, and then ask for help.

【设计说明】 听课文录音进行跟读,引导学生关注语音、语调,同时检测学生对文本的理解状况。

Step 2　Robin's advice (6 mins)

Activity 1：Talk about the new schedule

Listen to Robin's advice and talk about Wu Yifan's new schedule.

T：Does Wu Yifan like sports? Is it good?

(The teacher plays the recording：Robin：I give you some advice.)

T：This is Robin's advice.

(Recording：Robin：Here is a new schedule for you. Students read this sentence. Then the teacher shows Robin's schedule.)

T：Wu Yifan, what do you have on Mondays and Fridays?

S1：(I have a football class.)

T：What do you have on Tuesdays，Thursdays and Saturdays?

S2：(I have a ping-pong class.)

T：What do you have on Wednesdays?

S3：(I have a basketball class.)

T：What do you have on Sundays?

S4：(I have a Kungfu class.)

T：From Monday to Friday，Wu Yifan plays sports every day.

Robin：You should play sports every day.（Students practice this sentence.）That is the advice.（Students practice this sentence at last.）

【设计说明】 帮助学生更加深入地理解 Robin 给 Wu Yifan 的时间表,使他们不仅知道新时间表是怎样安排的,还能发现 Robin 给出这个新时间表的原因。

Activity 2：Retell

Retell the schedule given by Robin.

T：This is Wu Yifan's new schedule. Now，suppose you were Wu Yifan, please retell the new schedule.

Ss：(Robin gives some advice. Now，I have a football class on Mondays and Fridays. I have a ping-pong class on Tuesdays，Thursdays and Saturdays. I have a basketball class on Wednesdays. I have a Kungfu class on Sundays.)

【设计说明】 文本的复述检测了学生对课文的掌握和理解情况,锻炼了学生的语言组织能力,为下文的写做活动做铺垫。

Step 3　Writing part (6 mins)

Activity 1：Choose the right handwriting

Choose the right handwriting of sentence，tell the reason why A and B are wrong. Then the teacher shows the tips one by one.

Let's write
选出正确的一句

Tip 6：1.注意 _f g j p q y_ 书写。
2.词词之间隔开小写字母a的距离。
3.句子开头要大写。

A　I have afootball class.

B　i have a football　class.

♡　I have a football class.

【设计说明】 让学生在活动中练习英语句子一线格的书写,注重一线格书写字体、间距等要点。

Activity 2：Complete the conversation

Complete the dialogue according to the schedule that Robin gives to Wu Yifan.

The teacher will show the tips and check the sentences with students.

Let's write p19
1. 独立完成对话，
   注意书写格式。
2. 同桌互相检查。

Tip6: 1. 注意 f g j p q y 书写
2. 词词之间隔开小写字母a的距离。
3. 句子开头要大写。

Student: Wu Yifan   Teacher: Robin

| Mon. | Tues. | Wed. | Thur. | Fri. | Sat. | Sun. |

Look at the schedule above and complete the dialogue below.

Sarah: What do you have on Mondays?

Wu Yifan: I have a football class.

Sarah: What do you have on Tuesdays?

Wu Yifan: *I have a ping-pong class*.

Sarah: *What do you have on Wednesdays*?

Wu Yifan: I have a basketball class.

【设计说明】 本活动旨在检测学生对文本中时间表的理解和掌握，要求在教师的指导下完成 Robin 建议部分的写作，培养学生的信息整合能力。

Stage 3   Post-reading (7 mins)

Step 1   David's schedule (2 mins)

The teacher introduces a new friend David to students, presenting his schedule and asking students to evaluate it.

T: We have a friend. He is active. He is David. (The teacher shows the passage with the background music.)

Passage

David: I like basketball.

David plays basketball on Mondays. David plays basketball on Tuesdays.

David plays basketball on Wednesdays. David plays basketball on Thursdays.

David plays basketball on Fridays. David plays basketball on Saturdays.

David plays basketball on Sundays.

T: What do you think of David's schedule?

S1: (He always plays sports.)

T：Is it good or not?

S2：(It isn't good.)

T：Can you give some advice to him?

S2：(He shouldn't often play sports.)

T：David shouldn't always play sports. He should keep balance.

【设计说明】 在介绍 David 的过程中让学生认识到过度运动也是不合理的。

Step 2　Students' weekend schedules (5 mins)

Work in pairs to make weekend schedules for themselves.

T：David doesn't have a balanced sports schedule. How would you reasonably arrange your
weekend schedule? Do you often play sports on weekend?

S1：...

S2：...

T：Discuss with your partner and write down your advice on your weekend schedule and
then share with us. (The teacher shows an example and a word bank for them.)

Let's write

My advice

A：What do you often do on the weekend?

B：I often _____ . Sometimes I _____ .

A：_____ on _____ s?

B：_____ .

A：Do you often _____ on _____ ?

B：Yes, I do. /No, I don't.

A：Good! You should insist on. /Oh, no! You should play sports every day.

Word Bank

play football	football class
play basketball	basketball class
play ping-pong	ping-pong class
run	running class
do Kungfu	Kungfu class
......	......

【设计说明】 这一活动可以锻炼学生的合作能力、语言组织能力和写作能力,并引导学生学
会合理分配运动时间和学习时间。

六、 作业布置

1. Finish writing *My advice*.
2. Read the passage aloud on p19 for 10 - 15 minutes.

【设计说明】 写作作业是本节课的知识点的综合运用,可以巩固学生的语言知识;朗读课文可以增强学生语音语调的训练,提高学生的口语能力。

七、 板书设计

```
                    PEP5 Unit2 My week

                    B Read and write

                1. What do you have on…s?           schedule

What do you       I have…                            tired

often do…?      2. What do you often do on…s/the weekend?    play sports

                  I often…Sometimes I …              should

                3. Do you often…?                    every day

                  Yes, I do. /No, I don't.
```

【设计说明】 主板书的左边为重点句型,右边为重点单词,可帮助学生完成课堂的阅读和写作,整理课堂知识点。

八、 教学反思

本节课属于小学高年级英语读写教学课。本节课中,教师从教材文本出发,基于教材内在的情境创设了多样化的教学活动,引发学生思考,在师生真实交流中促进学生能力的发展。本课有三个基本的亮点:(一)强化基本的阅读技能和写作技能。本节课中,学生运用扫读和跳读概括了文章大意并找出特定问题的答案,运用已学的句型和单词完成写作任务,学生的阅读技能和写作技能都得到有效训练。(二)提升学生的思维品质。通过判断对错、复述时间表等活动,培养学生理解层次的思维能力;通过评价 Wu Yifan 和 David 的时间表,培养评价层次的思维能力;根据他人的建议自行设计合理的时间表,培养创造层次的思维能力。由易到难,循序渐进,逐步提高学生的高层次思维能力。(三)养成良好的运动习惯。从一开始老师的热爱运动到 Wu Yifan 的厌恶运动再到 David 的过度运动,整堂课都在给学生呈现合理运动的重要性,使学生通过良好的情感体验培养良好的生活运动习惯。

(教学设计者:江南实验小学　吴芳芳)

说课案例八(语音课)

PEP 2 Unit 5 It's Fun to Jump A Let's spell

微课

Hello, everyone. I'm Christine. It's my great honor to present my lesson plan here. The lesson I will present is from PEP 2 Unit 5 *Do you like pears?* Part A *Let's spell*.

I. Analysis

Firstly, let's focus on the teaching material. The content of this lesson is from PEP 2 Unit 5 *Do you like pears?* Part A *Let's spell*. It consists of three parts: Listen, repeat and chant; Read, listen and number; Listen and write. In order to help students have a better understanding of the vowel "u" in context, I will use the picture book *It's Fun to Jump*. In the lesson, students are supposed to perceive, experience, conclude and apply the phoneme /ʌ/(u), spell words with the letter u(/ʌ/) and write the key words, and improve their ability of reading and writing step by step.

Secondly, let's focus on the learners. The learners are in Grade 3. They are active and curious about new things. So picture book, chant and role-play will attract their attention. Moreover, they have learned consonants and vowels (a, e, i, o). And they have formed some spelling habits and gained some spelling skills. The above mentioned are advantages for students to learn the letter "u".

II. Statement

Based on the analysis of the teaching material and learners, here come the learning objectives. For communicative competence, firstly, students will be able to know the phoneme /ʌ/(u) by listening to and observing the key words; secondly, they will be able to spell these words *fun*, *run*, *duck*, *sun*, *under*, then spell and read more words with the same rules; thirdly, students can write down these key words correctly. For cognitive and thinking ability, they can observe, understand and apply the phoneme /ʌ/(u). For social-cultural awareness: students will be happy to imitate the phoneme, have the courage to spell the words, and have interest in learning English.

In this lesson, we have two teaching focuses: the understanding and use of the phoneme /ʌ/(u) and the writing of the key words *fun*, *run*, *duck*, *sun*, *under*. However, students will meet with some difficulties in this lesson. The major one is that students are supposed to observe and know the phoneme /ʌ/(u) by themselves and then use it. Considering all of these mentioned, I will adopt PWP teaching mode. Also, CAI and worksheets will be used as the props to facilitate my teaching.

III. Description

Now, the description of my teaching procedures. I will follow three steps: Lead-in, Learn to use , Read and act.

Let's begin with Step 1 — Lead-in. There are two activities: "Watch and say" and "Get to know Gus". In Activity 1, students will watch a video about alphablocks. When they are watching, they will speak out the phonemes of 26 letters. This video can activate students' previous knowledge and get them ready for the lesson. Then comes Activity 2 "Get to know Gus". There are three letters on the PPT: g, u, s. Students will try to spell like: /g/, /ʌ/, /s/, /gʌs/. Then I will introduce the boy Gus to students. "Hello! I'm Gus. I can jump. Fun! Fun! Fun!" Then I will say, "Gus can jump. Look at this picture. He can jump over the ..." Students will answer together, "Duck". This activity is to let students have a general idea of the situation. What's more, the key word "duck" lays a foundation for the next step.

Now, Step 2 "Learn to use". There are four activities in Step 2, Let's chant, Make a word, Read, listen and number, Listen and write.

We will talk about Activity 1 first. In the beginning, I will show a chant about the duck and ask students a question "Which sound do you hear most?" Some of them may say /ʌ/. The second question is "Can you find some words with/ʌ/?" The students may answer like *duck*, *sun*, *under* and *run*. This is to help students focus on these key words. Then, students will listen and repeat after the sound "duck, duck, run, run, under, under, sun, sun". So they can practice the phoneme /ʌ/(u). After repeating, students will focus on letter "u" and guess how "u" pronounces here. Then they will watch a video about letter "u". This is to input native sound. Then I will say, "We know 'u' pronounces/ʌ/, can you spell these words?" Volunteers will stand up and spell. For example, /d/, /ʌ/, /k/, /dʌk/. It aims to consolidate the phoneme /ʌ/(u). After spelling, students will open their book and turn to Page 50. They will listen, repeat and chant. This is the first part in the textbook. It aims to make students' spoken English more native and accurate.

This is all about Activity 1. Now, Activity 2, "Make a word". First, I will show students this slide and ask them to make words with the letters and spell these words. Some words are from Activity 3, for example, *cut*. So students can get familiar with these words and be well prepared for Activity 3. Some words are from the story *It's Fun to Jump*, for example, *bus*. So they can understand and read the story much better.

Now, let's move to Activity 3, "Read, listen and number". This is the second part of the textbook. Firstly, students will read the words on their books. Then they will listen and number these words on their books. This activity aims to improve their reading ability and listening ability.

The last activity in Step 2 is "Listen and write". This is a little different from the third part in the textbook. Look! This is the content in the book. And this is my design. It seems more difficult than the former. But I'm sure students can finish it. The sound will go like "I'm a duck. /d/, /ʌ/, /k/, /dʌk/". The students will write down the word "duck" on their worksheets. After they finish all the words, students will exchange their worksheets with partners. Then they will look at the blackboard and check with me. I will say, "I'm a duck. /d/, /ʌ/, /k/, /dʌk/. I like to run. /r/, /ʌ/, /n/, /rʌn/. Under the sun. /ʌ/, /n/, /d/, /ə/, /ʌndə/. Attention, please. Here, 'U' is capitalized." Students will find that the first letter in a sentence should be capitalized. Then, I will go on, "Under the sun. /s/, /ʌ/, /n/, /sʌn/. It's fun. /f/, /ʌ/, /n/, /fʌn/." It is to improve the ability of writing. Also, it helps students develop the ability of self-evaluation. As a result, they can improve their independent learning.

This is all about Step 2. Now, let me present Step 3. There are two activities. They are "Read the story" and "Let's act". Firstly, I will ask a question, "Gus can jump over the duck. What else?" Then, I will present the sound of the story. The students will get interested in the story and they will try to listen carefully and find out the answer. If it's a little difficult, I will present the sound again. By listening, students can have a general idea of the story. And it can improve their listening ability. After listening, here comes a group work. The students will take out their worksheets and read the sentences in groups. They are the key sentences in the story. Students can choose sentences of different difficulty levels, which can guarantee their participation and build up their confidence. After the group work, students will listen and repeat the whole story sentence by sentence. So they will pay attention to the pronunciation and intonation. When they are reading, they can have a general understanding of the story. In a word, students can get ready for the next activity. Finally, here comes the output activity. Students will act out the story in groups. When they are acting, they will pay attention to the body language, tone and expression.

Group performance can develop students' ability of communication and cooperation. It can also arouse students' interest in English learning. Later, I will ask them a question, "Is it fun to jump?" Students will answer, "Yes. It's fun to jump." Then, I will write down the title *It's Fun to Jump*.

IV. Exposition

A good blackboard design can help students get key information clearly and quickly. So I will make a design like this: The title of the lesson will be on the top. The key words will be on the left, while the other words will be on the right.

There are three kinds of homework. Students can choose one according to their own ability and interest. Homework 1 consolidates the content in the textbook. Homework 2 activates students' interest in reading. Homework 3 encourages students to learn by themselves.

V. Reflection

Well, on the whole, students can achieve their learning objectives step by step in this class, and there are three shining points of my lesson. Firstly, the picture book *It's Fun to Jump is* used in the class. It can arouse the students' interest in learning the letter "u". Secondly, during the learning process, students are supposed to perceive, experience, conclude and apply the phoneme /ʌ/(u) by themselves, and also spell the words with the letter u(/ʌ/). It can enhance their ability of independent learning. Thirdly, this lesson is student-centered. Different kinds of activities can help the students to develop their ability of thinking, communication and cooperation.

That's all. Thanks for your attention. Goodbye!

(说课稿撰写者：温州市百里路小学　胡夏子)

附：教学设计

PEP 2 Unit 5 It's Fun to Jump Part A Let's spell

一、教学背景

1. 教材分析

本课时教学内容选自新版人教版《英语》三年级下册 Unit 5 *It's Fun to Jump* Part A

Let's spell。本课时教材内容共分为三个板块：Listen，repeat and chant，Read，listen and number 和 Listen and write。为了让学生更好地在情境中学习语音，本课将对教材内容做适当修改并且融入绘本 *It's Fun to Jump*。通过学习，学生能够主动感知、体验、归纳和运用字母"u"的音素/ʌ/，拼读含有 u(/ʌ/)的词汇并且拼写重点词汇，培养见词能读和听音能写的能力，并能够进行绘本阅读。

2. 学情分析

三年级的小学生生性活泼，对新事物富有好奇心。因此，教师应努力创设浸入式、自然的学习环境，充分利用 chant、绘本等资源吸引学生注意力，引导学生进行模仿、表演。经过半年多的学习，学生已基本掌握辅音字母以及"a，e，i，o"4 个短元音的发音规则，初步养成拼读的意识和习惯。

二、 教学目标

1. 语言交际目标

（1）能够通过听歌谣和例词，观察例词中共有的字母，知道字母 u 在单词中发/ʌ/音。

（2）能够拼读出符合发音规则的单词 fun，run，duck，sun，under，并根据发音拼读出更多符合规则的单词。

（3）能够在四线三格中正确书写词汇 fun，run，duck，sun，under。

（4）能理解 chant 和绘本故事的大意，并且在仿读、指读、表演的过程中培养语感。

2. 思维认知目标

（1）能积极和组员合作，共同完成学习单上的学习任务。

（2）能通过观察、思考得出发音规律并进行运用。

3. 社会文化目标

在学习过程中乐于模仿元音字母 u 的发音，敢于拼读，对英语学习有兴趣。

三、 教学重难点

1. 教学重点

（1）在情境中感知、体验、归纳"u"的音素/ʌ/，并且拼读出符合该发音规则的单词。

（2）在四线三格中正确书写词汇 fun，run，duck，sun，under。

2. 教学难点

通过自身的观察和思考得出"u"的音素/ʌ/并且进行运用。

四、 教学准备

PPT，学习单

五、 教学过程

Step 1　Lead-in（5 mins）

Activity 1：Watch and say

Watch the video and speak out the phonemes of 26 letters with the video.

【设计说明】 视频热身，吸引学生注意力并且复习 26 个字母音素。

Activity 2：Get to know Gus

Teacher presents three letters "g，u，s" on the PPT. Students speak out the word "Gus" according to phonics. Then teacher presents the self-introduction of Gus.

T：What does Gus say? Let's listen.

> **Listening script**
>
> Hello! I'm Gus. I can jump. Fun! Fun! Fun!

Then teacher presents a picture from the picture book.

T：Gus can jump. Look at this picture. He can jump over the ...

Ss：He can jump over the duck.

【设计说明】 引出绘本故事主角 Gus，让学生先整体感知语境，对本课学习内容有所预测；借用绘本插图引出 duck，为下一个环节呈现 chant 做好铺垫。

Step 2　Learn to use（20 mins）

Activity 1：Let's chant

A：Listen and find

Listen to the chant and try to find out the sound they hear most.

T：Here is a chant about the duck. Now，let's listen.

> **Listening script**
>
> Run duck，run! Run duck，run! Under the sun. Under the sun. Run duck，run! Run! Run! Run!

T：Please tell me which sound do you hear most?

S1：/ʌn/.

S2：/ʌ/.

Then，students try to find out the words with/ʌ/like "sun，run，duck，under".

T：Can you find some words with/ʌ/?

S1：Sun.

S2：...

【设计说明】 进行语篇的整体输入,使学生在语篇中初步感知字母"u"的发音,培养学生听的能力。从学生发音练习中引出本课重点词汇,由篇到词,使本课学习内容更加清晰。

B：Listen and repeat

Listen to the words and repeat one by one.

(Tape script：Duck, duck. Run, run. Under, under. Sun, sun)

【设计说明】 学生在听和模仿的过程中练习字母"u"的发音,为下一个环节自主发现"u"的发音规律做好铺垫。

C：Observe and guess

Find out the same letter among these words and guess the phoneme of this letter. Then, the teacher presents a video to check the phoneme of this letter.

T：Now, look at these words. What's the same letter?

Ss："u".

T：Here, "u" says ...

S1："u" says /ʌ/.

T：Now, let's watch the video to check.

【设计说明】 由词到音,引导学生主动观察、思考,培养学生的思维能力和学习的主动性。充分利用视频"磨耳朵",有助于学生学习地道的语音。

D：Let's spell

Teacher presents these words on the PPT：*duck*, *run*, *under*, *sun*. Some students stand up and spell these words. Other students and teacher listen carefully and check.

Let's spell

d-u-ck→duck

r-u-n→run

s-u-n→sun

u-n-d-er→under

【设计说明】 新知呈现之后马上进行巩固练习,促进学生知识内化。

E：Listen and repeat

Students open the book，listen to the recording and repeat. After reading the words, they chant with the recording.

Chant

Run duck，run! Run duck，run!

Under the sun，under the sun，

Run duck，run! Run! Run! Run!

【设计说明】 回归教材"Listen，repeat and chant"板块，学生在模仿录音的过程中巩固新知，学习地道的语音、语调，培养语感。

Activity 2：Make a word

Make up words with the given letters individually.

T：Now，look at these three letters：c，u，t．Can you make them into a word?

S1：/k/，/ʌ/，/t/，/kʌt/．

Make a word

Tips:
1. 伸出手指
2. 声音响亮，注意力集中

t	b	s	b
t	n	c	t
f	n	<u>m</u>	d
j	m	p	g

（注：表格中 c、u 与 t 组成 cut）

【设计说明】 拼读的单词选自教材 Listen and number 板块和绘本 *It's Fun to Jump*。此环节一举两得，既可以培养学生"见词能拼"的能力和良好的拼读习惯，又可以为下一环节的听音标序和拓展环节的绘本阅读扫清障碍。

Activity 3：Read，listen and number

A：Let's read

Read the second part of their textbooks：duck，cut，run，fun，under，up.

B：Let's listen and number

Listen to the recording and number the words on their books.

【设计说明】 回归教材"Read，listen and number"板块。将该板块内容分解为两个层次：指读单词和听音标序，缓慢加大难度，逐步培养学生对词汇的认读能力和听音辨词的能力。

Activity 4：Listen and write

Take out their worksheets，listen to the recording and write down the words. After that，exchange their worksheets with partners and check under the teacher's help.

Listen and write

I'm a ========.

I like to ========.

======== the ========.

It's so ========.

【设计说明】 在语篇中听音写单词,如 I'm a duck。/d/, /ʌ/, /k/, /dʌk/,培养学生"听音能写"的能力。引导学生关注 Under 的 U 要大写,为学生良好的书写习惯打下基础。学生之间相互评价,把评价的主动权还给学生。

Step 3　Read and act (9 mins)

Activity 1：Read the story

A：Listen and answer

Listen to the recording of the story，and then try to find out the answer.

T：What else can Gus jump over?

S1：Gus can jump over the bus.

S2：Gus can jump over the sun.

【设计说明】 整体输入故事,让学生初步感知故事大意;听录音回答问题,培养学生获取关键信息的能力。

B：Read aloud

Choose at least one sentence from the box based on difficulty level，and then read aloud by themselves.

Read aloud

☆	1. Jump over the **duck**. 2. Jump over the **bus**. 3. Jump over the **sun**.
☆☆	1. Jump over the **cups**.
☆☆☆	1. Jump over the **drum**. 2. Jump over the **mushroom**. （fi**sh**, class**room**)

【设计说明】 拼读是促进学生英语阅读的"拐杖"。由音到词,由词到句,逐步培养学生的阅

读能力。自主选择不同难度的句子,降低了任务的难度,保护了学生学习的积极性,也为下一环节的仿读以及表演扫清障碍。

C:Listen and repeat

Listen to the recording and repeat the whole story sentence by sentence.

【设计说明】 回归语篇,让学生对绘本内容有一个完整的体验,加深理解。引导学生模仿正确的语音、语调,提高学生朗读的准确度和流利度,有助于学生更加生动形象地表演绘本故事。

Activity 2:Let's act

Act out the story in groups,and pay attention to the pronunciation and intonation.

T: Now,please take out your worksheet. Work in group of four. Let's act.

【设计说明】 在小组合作中,学生以自己喜欢的方式表演绘本故事。本活动给予学生充足的想象空间,激发学生的表演欲望以及对英语绘本的热爱。

六、 作业布置 (1 min)

1. Read p50 for 5 times.

2. Read the story *It's Fun to Jump* to partners.

3. Collect more words with u(/ʌ/) (at least 5 words).

【设计说明】 作业布置充分考虑学生的个体差异,尽可能让每一位学生完成适合自己的作业。作业 1、2 为巩固类作业,旨在帮助学生更好地巩固教材内容或绘本内容。作业 3 为拓展类作业,旨在鼓励学生主动学习,扩充学生的词汇量。

七、 板书设计

It's Fun to Jump

duck   run   up
                           cup
              sun   cut
                           bus
under   mushroom
              fun   drum

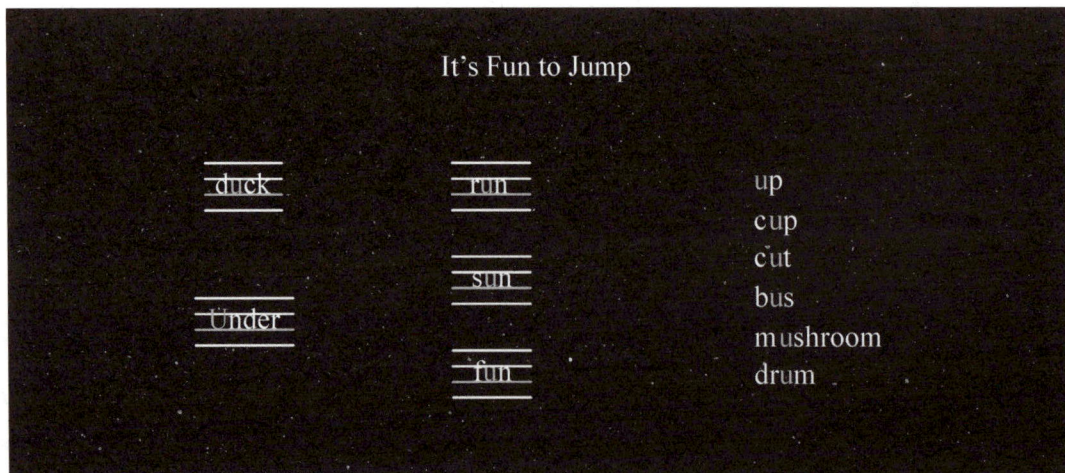

【设计说明】 板书设计简单明了,重难点突出,有助于学生回顾本课的主要知识点。本课的标题在师生互动的过程中得出,让学生印象深刻。黑板左边的为本课的重点词汇,要求学生在四线三格上正确书写。黑板右边为本课的拓展词汇,要求学生会认读。

附学习单

Worksheet for PEP2 Unit5 A. Let's spell
It's Fun to Jump

1. Listen and write

Steps:
1.听音写词
2.同桌交换评价
   3☆:字母拼写正确,书写规范
   2☆:字母拼写有误/书写不规范
注意:句首字母大写可多得1☆

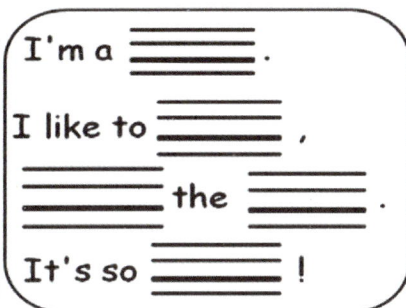

I'm a _____.
I like to _____,
_____ the _____.
It's so _____!

2. Read aloud

温馨小提示:
根据自身的意愿选择某个难度值的句子,每人至少一句。
注:星星的数量代表难度值

★	1. Jump over the <u>duck</u>. 2. Jump over the <u>bus</u>. 3. Jump over the <u>sun</u>.
★★	1. Jump over the <u>cups</u>.
★ ★★	1. Jump over the <u>drum</u>. 2. Jump over the <u>mushroom</u>.

3. Let's act

温馨小提示:
合作表演,形式不限,注意动作、语气、神态哦。

It's Fun to Jump
It's fun to... jump,jump,jump.
Jump over the duck.
Jump over the drum.
Jump over the cups.
Jump over the mushroom.
Jump over the bus.
Jump over the sun.
Oops!
Up! Up! Up!
It's fun to jump.

八、教学反思

1. 创设情境,增加课堂整体性和趣味性

本课充分利用绘本 *It's Fun to Jump* 创设整体情境,让学生在情境中学习和运用语言。从课堂一开始的认识主人公 Gus,到巩固环节的 Make a word,再到拓展环节的绘本阅读,课堂始终围绕 *It's Fun to Jump* 推进。此外,绘本的运用增加了学生的感官体验,丰富学生的语言体验和情感体验,使语音课不再那么枯燥乏味。

2. 循序渐进,提升语言学习和运用能力

本课通过合理设计使学生有序地、渐进性地达成学习目标。通过 Listen and find, Listen and repeat, Observe and guess, Make a word 等活动让学生经历自主感知语言、体验语言、得出规律、运用规律的学习过程。学生的知识逐步内化为"见词能拼,听音能写"的能力,从而使自然拼读成为辅助学生英语阅读的一个拐杖。

3. 任务驱动,促进学生自主合作学习

本课以学习单为载体,让学生明确自身任务或小组任务,引导学生进行自主合作学习。在 Listen and write 活动中,学生完成书写后进行相互评价。教师把评价的主动权充分交还给学生。在 Read and act 活动中,学生先后经历小组合作朗读句子和小组合作表演故事。他们的交际能力与合作能力得到了充分的培养。

（教学设计者：温州市上戍小学　郏婕婕）

说课案例九(复习课)

PEP 5 At Willow Primary School Recycle 1

Hello, everyone! I'm Li Hao from Wenzhou Guangchanglu Primary School. It is my great honor to be here sharing my lesson plan with you. The lesson I am going to share is a revision lesson from Recycle One, PEP 5.

微课

Ⅰ. Analysis

First, let's come to the analysis of the teaching material and learning conditions. The content of this lesson is the first period of Recycle One in PEP 5. The topic of it is about Chen Jie's visit to Willow Primary School in the UK where she met different people, had different school schedules and made new friends. This lesson is to help my students review the key words and sentence patterns "What's he/she like? He/She is ..." "What do you have on ...? We have ... on ..." "My favorite ... is ...." in language contexts.

As for the students, they are from Grade Five who have already had two-year English learning experience. They have obtained some basic learning strategies. And they have known how to use key words and expressions. Meanwhile, they have learned basic phonics in previous units. So in this lesson I will guide them to review and to summarize what they have learned.

II. Statement

Here come the learning objectives. First, for language competence, students will be able to use the sentence patterns "What's he/she like? He/She is ..." "What do you have on ...? We have ... on ..." to make a description of their teachers as well as the school schedule in a day. Second, for cognitive ability, by the end of the lesson, students will be able to improve their memorizing ability by using mind maps to sort out and memorize the descriptive words of people's appearance and personality. Also, students will be able to improve their understanding and analyzing abilities by generalizing and summarizing what they have learned with the hints. Third, for social-cultural awareness, students will be happy to describe their teachers, classmates and favorite subjects. What's more, they will experience the joy by using English to communicate.

As a revision lesson, the teaching focus is to train students to use these useful words and expressions in new contexts. However, it's a difficult point for students to reorganize, summarize and use the language points.

III. Description

Now I am going to show you the teaching procedures. I will divide it into four steps.

The first step is warming up and revision. There are two activities in this step. In Activity One, we will play the game of concentration. I will show students the words about appearance and personality. Students will be asked to memorize those words. They will try to speak them out. The more, the better. This section aims to review the words they have learned in the previous units.

In Activity Two, students will be asked to use the words reviewed in Activity One to describe me. Sentences like "Mr. Li is .../He is ..." will be used in this activity. This activity is efficient for them to go over the words and expressions they have learned in Unit One. Considering that my students are always happy to talk about their English teacher, the question "Where do I work?" will be put forward. They will answer, "You work in GCL Primary School." Thus, the phrase "primary school" is perfectly elicited. It will pave a way for the next step.

After eliciting the phrase "primary school", let's move on to Step Two "revision and practice". There are four activities in this step. Activity One is "Let's match". I will ask students where Willow Primary School is. And they will try to guess the answer with the sentence "Is it in ...?" After guessing, students will listen to the recording and find out the answer. The guessing question will draw their attention to listen and to get the answer

"Chen Jie is visiting Willow Primary School in the UK". The school in the UK will arouse students' curiosity as they may wonder the differences between a British school and a Chinese school.

Activity Two is to talk about the teachers. The pictures of Chen Jie and David will be shown on PPT. I will ask students to guess what they are talking about. There are two options for them to tick, *A. The school B. Teachers*. The guessing game will activate their interest and guide them to focus on the key information. This activity will involve all students to predict the story, to listen to the dialogue and to check their answers through pictures on PPT. After students tick the answer *B. Teachers*, I will ask them three questions *"Which teacher is David introducing to Chen Jie? What's she like? Is she strict?"* Students will answer, *"His Chinese teacher, Ms Wang. She's kind. Yes, sometimes."* respectively. Then they will make up a dialogue based on the mind map about Ms. Zhang and the written dialogue on PPT with my help. It will help them to review the main sentences and summarize the main sentence patterns. Thus it will lay a good foundation for the next activity. After the dialogue, more teachers in Willow Primary School will be shown on PPT. My students will be asked to speak out their names "Ms Brown, Mr Smith, Mr. Kelly, Mr. Reed". Here the vowels **"ow, i, ee, e"** will be guided to pronounce according to the spelling rules. After that, students will listen to the introduction of a teacher, Ms. Brown. Then, I will summarize key words and sentences together with students according to the mind map on PPT. Under the dialogue model I present, students will work in pairs to make up a dialogue with the words and sentences they've learned according to the mind map.

Activity Three is to talk about their favorite classes. Chen Jie and David are in the classroom. Two of David's classmates, Dean and Jean, are introduced to Chen Jie. Here I will ask students to spell the letter combination "ea". By looking at the picture, I will start a conversation with students *"What's Jean doing? Can you guess what her favorite class is?"* Students will try to observe the pictures to get the answer. I will invite three students to answer these questions. To check the correct answers, I will ask them to listen and circle them. Here, the answer *"Jean's favorite class is art."* will pave a way for the next activity.

Activity Four is to talk about their classes from Monday to Friday. David's schedule will be shown to students. Here some classes are missing in David's Monday schedule. In order to make the listening practice easier, first I will ask students a question *"Can you guess what classes they have on Monday?"* Students will guess the answer with the sentence pattern "Maybe they have ..." After guessing, I will ask students to listen and fill in the schedule on Monday. Then we will check the answers together. After that, I will ask students to listen again and fill in the schedule from Tuesday to Friday. Here it will help students review the words "classes, days", and also the phrases they have learned in Unit Two.

After listening practice, David's complete schedule will be given to students. They will read the schedule and then try to judge if the four sentences given are correct or not. This exercise is taken from Page 33. I will ask students to grasp some key information from the schedule to finish this task. In this way, students will learn to find key information for reading comprehension. Also their critical thinking and observing ability will be enhanced. What's more, key words and expressions will be much practiced during this process.

The third step is summarization and extension. Here are two activities to facilitate the full mastery of language points. In Activity One, I will ask students to summarize what information Chen Jie got during the day. Students will talk about Chen Jie's day according to the mind map given. They will talk about teachers' appearance, school subjects and friends' favorite classes at Willow Primary School. I will try to guide students to sum up and reorganize the words and sentence patterns in this activity. Students will answer with declarative sentences and I will write down the key words on the board. Chen Jie has written a diary about the information she got at Willow Primary School. So students will be asked to read Chen Jie's diary and to underline the key sentences according to the key words on the board. Students will analyze the text from words to sentences and then from sentences to passage. By the end of Step 3, students will be asked to work together in a group to write a diary about their own school, imitating Chen Jie's diary. Writing is not easy to fifth grade students, but with the mind map they made in former activity, it will be easier. So after writing, a representative of a group will present her diary to all of us. These activities aim to train students' ability of reorganizing key words and expressions and at the same time, students' communicative ability and reading comprehension will also be enhanced.

IV. Exposition

As I think, reading is as important as writing in consolidating what students learn in class. So I will design the following homework for this lesson, which aims to further consolidate what they have learned.

1. Review Unit 1 and Unit 3 once by reading.

2. Finish your diary and share it with your friends.

At last, I would like to share my board design with you. First, it presents a mind map, which helps students have a clear understanding of the learning material. Second, it shows some useful words and sentence patterns to facilitate students' communication and writing.

V．Reflection

Now I have presented the whole lesson. Here comes my brief reflection on this lesson. Firstly，the class is student-centered，with lots of time for students to think and to talk. And a mind map is designed to help them summarize and reorganize the key words and sentences. Secondly，this lesson focuses on skills and strategies of learning. For example，while training their writing ability，students are asked to imitate the way Chen Jie wrote her diary. It will facilitate the writing ability of the students. Thirdly，the lesson attaches great significance to students' thinking ability，with lots of activities and questions for learners to think more widely and deeply.

That's all for my lesson presentation. Thanks a lot!

（说课稿撰写者：温州市广场路小学　李浩）

附：教学设计

一、 教学背景

1. 教材分析

本课选自人教版《英语》五年级上册 Recycle 1 的第一课时。教材以 Chen Jie 参观英国的 Willow Primary School 的过程中，遇到的人和交谈的事为主线。本课结合了第一单元 What's he/she like? He/She is ... 和第二单元 What do you have on ... ? We have ... 的相关知识，融合了第三单元的 My favourite food 中的 favourite 来联系课程，如 My favourite class is ... 等句式来展开复习，让学生在完整的、连贯的语言情境中复习核心词汇和句型。

2. 学情分析

五年级的学生经过两年的英语学习，已经掌握了一定的学习方法。到 Recycle 课时的时候，学生已经积累了前三单元的核心词汇和句型。因此，本节课教师可着重引导学生回顾和整合旧知，最后进行整体输出。通过两年多的学习，学生已掌握了一些简单的自然拼读法，能够听懂简单的英语音频，乐于在生活中解决实际问题。教师可以利用学生的这个特点，在语音复习方面，把自主权交给学生；在听力复习方面，重在引导；在输出方面，以实际生活为导向，使学生"学以致用"。

二、 教学目标

1. 语言交际目标：

（1）在语境中熟练地运用已学句型 What's he/she like? He/She is ... 和 What do you have on ...? We have ... on ... 对熟悉的老师和一天的课程安排作简单的描述。

（2）综合运用本课已学知识 What's he/she like? He/She is ... 和 What do you have on ...? We have ... on ...，完成本课的听录音完成课程表，说一说自己的老师和朋友，读课程表完成判断及仿写日记等任务。

2. 思维认知目标：

（1）学生能够利用思维导图对描述人物外貌和性格特征的词汇进行梳理记忆，提升记忆层面的认知能力。

（2）学生能够通过教师给予的提示对所学知识进行归纳总结，从而提高理解与分析层面的认知能力。

3. 情感态度价值观目标：

（1）乐于用英语描述自己的老师、同学和自己最喜爱的课程。

（2）通过复习巩固，体验在用熟练的语言与学生分享有关自己的老师、同学和自己喜爱的课程等信息时获得的快乐。

三、 教学重难点

1. 教学重点：

在新的语境中较为自如地整理和运用已学句型 What's he/she like? He/She is ... 和 What do you have on ...? We have ... on ...，并在此基础上进行提升。

2. 教学难点：

学生能在课堂复习之中整理、归纳和熟练运用 strict/helpful/clever 等形容词和句型 What's he/she like? He/She is ... What do you have on ...? We have ... on ... 来谈论自己的老师和朋友等。

四、 教学准备

多媒体课件

五、 教学过程

Step 1　Warming-up and revision （4 mins）

Activity 1：Play a game：Concentration! （2 mins）

Students are asked to memorize the words about one's appearance and personality. Speak them out. The more, the better.

【设计说明】 利用思维导图复习第一单元描述人物外貌和性格特征的核心词汇,核心词汇可分为两类:一类用于描述人的外貌特征,另一类用于描述人的性格和个性特征,以帮助学生在复习课中对已学知识进行整理和归纳。

Activity 2:Let's say! (2 mins)

A. Students are asked to use these words to describe Miss Chen.

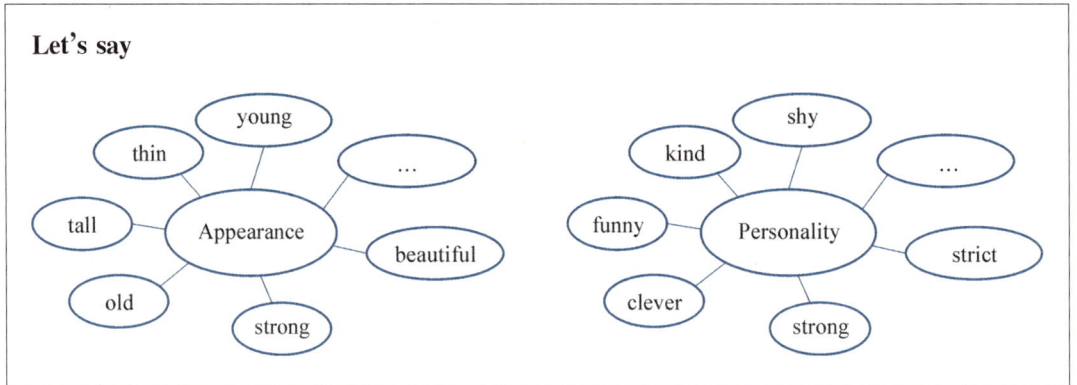

Let's say

Appearance: young, thin, tall, old, strong, beautiful, ...

Personality: shy, kind, funny, clever, strong, strict, ...

【设计说明】 激活旧知,在情境中运用词汇进行复习:学生不是简单地认读一遍单词,而是通过教师提供的词,思考说出 Miss Chen is . . ./She is . . . 等句子。在上一环节整理和归纳的基础上进行运用,培养学生归纳、整理、记忆等能力。

B. T:Where does Miss Chen work?

Ss:She works in Nanpu Primary School.   "i" [aɪ], "a"[ə], primary

【设计说明】 通过一个简单的问题,承接话题引出短语 Primary School,教授新词 primary,实现情境的自然过渡,让学生熟悉并了解这个词的意思,为下一环节的顺利进行做铺垫。

Step 2　Revision and practice　(18 mins)

Chen Jie is at Willow Primary School

Activity 1:Let's match (2 mins)

Answer the question:Where is Willow Primary School?

Ss:Is it in . . . ?

T:Listen and choose!

(Key sentence:Chen Jie is visiting Willow Primary School in the UK.)

【设计说明】 让学生猜学校所在的国家时复习了 Is it in . . .？ 这个一般疑问句,同时引导学生根据相关信息了解事情发生的地点,进而让学生利用听力来获取答案。提供中国、英国和美国这三个国家的国旗供学生选择,降低了听力难度,让学生明白 Chen Jie 参观的是英国的一所小学,而不是我们中国的学校,从而引起学生的好奇:这所学校跟国内的小学会不会有所不同呢?

Activity 2：Talk about the teachers (6 mins)

In Willow Primary School，Chen Jie meets her friend — David.

A. Guess：What are they talking about?

Then students listen and tick： A. The school. ☐ B. Teachers. ☑

(Key sentence：These are my teachers.)

【设计说明】 学生预测文本的发展,拓宽自己的思维。然后听力输入,出示 David 等六位老师的人物图片和句子,让学生获取答案。

B. Listen to the dialogue and find the answers.

T：Which teacher is David introducing to Chen Jie?

Ss：Ms Wang.

T：What's she like?

Ss：She is ...

T：Is she strict?

Ss：...

【设计说明】 学生在听力的基础上获取信息,师生进行对话,将这些信息记录在脑图中。学生回顾和整理 "Who's ....? /What's ... like? /Is he/she ...?" 句型,为下一环节做示范。

C. Know the teachers.

Know the teachers

Ms Brown Mr Smith Ms Zhang
Mr Reed Mr White Mr Kelly

T：Let's call the teachers together.

D. Work in pairs to make a dialogue with the words and sentences they have learned according to the mind map.

Make a dialogue

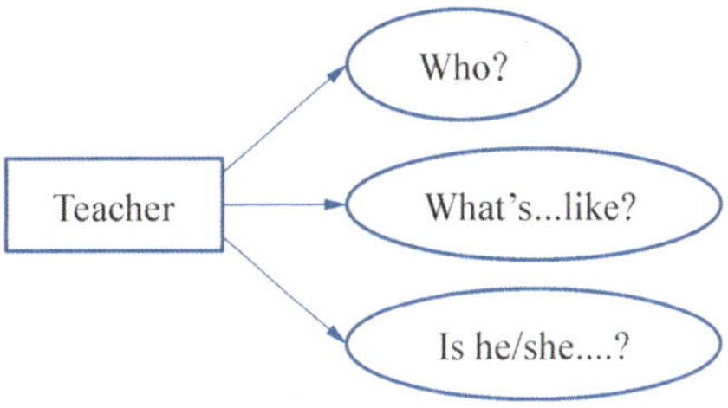

Ms Brown Mr Smith Ms Zhang
Mr Reed Mr White Mr Kelly

Teacher → Who?
Teacher → What's...like?
Teacher → Is he/she....?

【设计说明】 在创编对话前,先出示六位老师的称呼,语音渗透(ow[au],e[e],ee[iː]),突破难点。基于 Chinese teacher 的对话示范,学生可以根据图片以及各学科特点,整理第一单元的知识点进行运用——创编对话,进而内化语言知识,提升学生的语言表达能力。

Activity 3：Talk about their favourite classes (3 mins)

Chen Jie and David are in the classroom.

A. Students are asked to call David's classmates' names：Dean and Jean.

T：What's Jean doing?

Ss：She is drawing a picture.

T：Can you guess what her favourite class is?

Ss：She likes art best.

T：Do you know Dean's favourite class?

B. Listen and circle their favourite classes. （David，Jean and Dean）

【设计说明】 培养学生看图观察能力,并让学生能够通过 ea 组合拼读单词。学生通过图片预测再听,为下一环节讨论课程做了铺垫。

Activity 4：Talk about their classes from Mondays to Fridays（10 mins）

Talk about the classes David has from Monday to Friday according to his schedule.

A. Guess what classes David has on Mondays.

Days of the week / Time	Monday	Tuesday	Wednesday	Thursday	Friday
Morning	English	maths	science	English	reading
	science	English		computer class	maths
	?	science	maths	music	music
	?	computer class	English	maths	reading
Afternoon	?	music	science	science	
	reading			Chinese	English

Chen: David, what do you have on Mondays?
David: I have English, science, computer class and maths in the morning. In the afternoon, I have PE and reading class.
Chen: What's your favourite class?
David: I like English very much.

S1：Maybe they have Chinese in the morning.

S2：Maybe they have PE on Monday.

...

B. Listen and write down the classes on Mondays and then check the answer.

【设计说明】 填课程表的听力材料为三部分,若让学生一次性听,填空比较难。故教师引导学生先对星期一的课程进行猜测,在猜测的基础上进行听力。在听的过程中,教师教授听力技巧——找关键句,为接下去的两段听力做示范。

C. Listen and write down the classes from Tuesdays to Fridays.

【设计说明】 仿照上一环节的做题方法,在原有的基础上加深难度,让学生填写余下的课程,化难为简,从扶到放。本次活动使学生有效地完成了听和写的任务,整理了第二单元的知识点,复习了 days and classes。

D. Read and tick or cross.

【设计说明】 阅读总的课程表并判断对错,该题来自课本第33页的最后一大题。这个活动的设计培养了学生的阅读能力。学生在做题过程中学会了抓关键信息解题的能力。在校对环节让学生先读句子,对错误的句子进行订正,这些活动有利于提升孩子们的思维品质。

Step 3 Summarization and Extension (12 mins)

Activity 1:Summarize the information and draw your mind maps (7 mins)

A. T:Chen Jie's day at Willow Primary School is over.

Memorize the information they learned in this class in statement and the teacher writes down the key words on the blackboard.

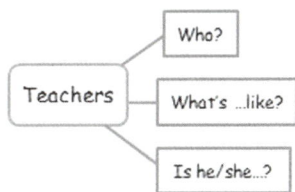

Teachers — Who? / What's …like? / Is he/she…?
tall/thin/beautiful…
kind/helpful/hard-working…

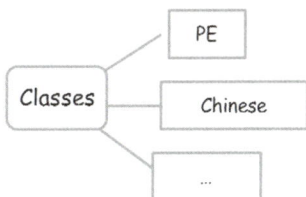

Classes — PE / Chinese / …
What do you have on…?
What's your favorite class?

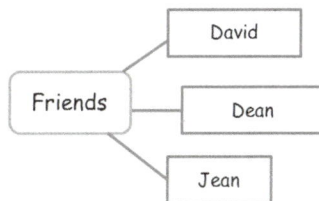

Friends — David / Dean / Jean
What's your favorite class?

【设计说明】 老师提问,学生回答。在师生的问答和教师的提示中,教师一步一步地引导学生利用板书,复习和归纳所学知识。

B. Students are asked to read Chen Jie's diary, underline the key sentences according to the mind maps.

Chen Jie's diary

Monday

I'm at Willow Primary School. It's big and clean. David is my good friend. His Chinese teacher is Ms Wang. She is very kind. But sometimes she is strict,too. Jean is his classmate. She likes Friday. On Fridays,they have reading class, maths, music,art and English. Jean's favourite class is art. She can draw well. I have great fun in Willow Primary School.

【设计说明】 让学生利用板书的关键词在阅读日记的过程中划出介绍 David 老师的名字、一天的课程安排以及同学最喜欢的课程等句子。从单词→句子→语篇,以点带面,让学生学会总结归纳学习句子的方法,并为接下来的知识运用做准备。

Activity 2：Imitate Chen Jie's diary and write a short passage (6 mins)

> *I'm at _____ Primary School. My _____ teacher is Ms Wang. _____ is very _____. But sometimes _____ is _____, too. _____ is my good classmate. _____ likes _____（一周中的某一天）. On _____, we have _____, _____ and _____. _____ favourite class is _____. I have great fun in my School.*

【设计说明】 在上一活动所完成的思维导图的基础上,以读、说促写,培养五年级孩子的书写能力。考虑到学生的写作能力,本课采用仿写方式,让学生体会写作技巧和语言的同时,降低了写作难度,让每位孩子参与其中。这一环节的仿写综合了孩子们的语言能力和英语学习的思维品质,借用思维导图来完成写作,是对孩子们的学习能力的一种要求。

六、 作业布置

A. Review Unit 1 and Unit 3 once by reading.

B. Finish your diary and share it with your friends.

【设计说明】 第一项作业是基础性作业。本课重点复习第一和第二单元的内容,故学生课后要再巩固。第二项作业是拓展性作业。学生将课上完成的日记进行完善及修改,并分享给同伴或朋友。这一环节使得学生的情感、态度、价值观目标得以充分地落实。

七、 板书设计

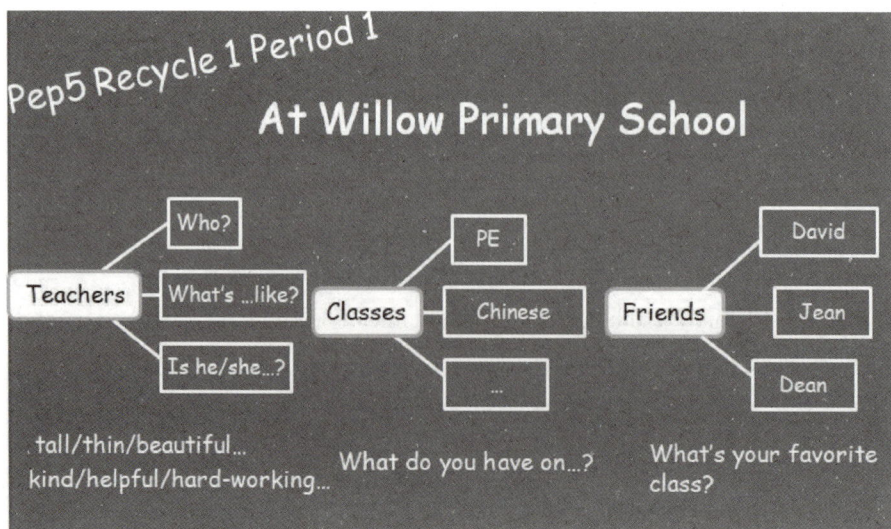

【设计说明】 本节课的语言知识点用板书呈现,有利于学生进一步掌握,并且学会整理知识的方法。

八、 教学反思

本课是一节复习课,重在培养学生对知识的整理和再运用的能力。故本课的设计从学生原有的知识水平出发,贯彻了由易到难、由浅入深、层层递进的教学原则。整体思路清晰,教学环节环环相扣,较好地实现了本课的教学目标。本课的设计亮点有:

1. 巧用思维导图,帮助学生整理和运用知识

本课从导入环节就借用思维导图,让学生自行复习所学的词汇。在语言操练阶段,引导学生根据思维导图的关键信息,整理和输出语言。在语言输出阶段,用思维导图来概括知识,学生学绘思维导图,并且根据导图内容进行模仿写作。在整个学习当中,思维导图有效地帮助了学生的学习。

2. 巧设活动任务,有助于培养自主学习能力

本课的活动设计遵循层层递进的方式来逐级地组织学生学习。在复习导入阶段,设计的词汇操练活动简单、机械,唤醒了学生的旧知。在语言操练阶段设计了听、说、读等环节,扎实、有效地让学生在整理和巩固知识的同时,掌握了基本的学习技能。在语言输出阶段设计的整理活动让学生熟知写作方式,自主模仿写作。

但本课的设计也有不足之处,如何能够更好地组织学生对知识的整理、概括与输出,还需进一步的思考。

（教学设计者：温州市南浦小学　陈欣欣）

说课案例十(对话表演课)

The Prefects
PEP 6 Unit 6 Work Quietly B Let's talk & Let's try

Hello，everyone. I'm Nicole. I'm glad to present my lesson plan here. The lesson I will present is from *New PEP 6 Unit 6 B Let's talk & Let's try*.

微课

Ⅰ. Analysis

The topic of this lesson is about the "rules"，and students are quite familiar with it. It aims to cultivate students' civic awareness by observing public rules. The passage has two

parts. The first part is pre-listening that tells students Tom and John are in the library. The second part is a dialogue of how Tom and John talk about rules in the library. Moreover, the gerund of a verb is firstly mentioned in this lesson.

My students are in Grade Five. They have accumulated some words about verbs, adjectives, places, etc. during two years' English learning. Moreover, most of them can learn cooperatively and independently. However, even though they have learnt the grammar "be+doing" before, the gerund of verb is new and difficult for them. They need more practice. Besides, students are eager to compete for the stars during this class.

II. Statement

Based on the above analysis, I set the following learning objectives: for communicative competence, firstly, by the end of the class, students will be able to listen, speak, read and understand the whole dialogue and the sentence patterns "... Keep ... clean. /Don't ...! / No ...! /... quietly" in a real communicative context. Secondly, students can read the whole dialogue aloud with correct pronunciation, intonation and stress as well. Thirdly students can make a new dialogue about rules for themselves. Lastly, students can make suggestions on public rules. For cognitive and thinking ability, students will be able to imitate and create according to the rules and the chant. So their abilities of knowledge transfer and creation will be improved. For social awareness, after this class, students will acquire civic awareness and enjoy the happiness from observing public rules.

Well, as a listening and speaking lesson, my whole lesson will focus on the sentence patterns like these in a context. There are also some teaching difficulties. So before this class, students in a group need to do some activities in a worksheet. Then I will use PPT and blackboard to make the teaching process go smoothly.

III. Description

My whole teaching process can be divided into three steps. They are revision and lead-in, presentation and practice, production.

In revision and lead-in step, firstly, I will show many places in the school by a mind-map. Then my students will be asked to have a brainstorm about places, such as "There is a playground", etc. Then they will find the prefects and describe them like "some of them are strict", etc. In this way, their previous knowledge will be activated which can lay a solid foundation for the following learning and create a language context.

In the next activity, students need to do some activities on the worksheet for reflection. They will read the rules, classify them and discuss in groups about the regulations. It aims to help them understand the sentence patterns "Don't …! No … !"

For the sake of fully practicing and understanding them, students will read more sentences and transform one to another, such as "Don't walk on the grass here!" to "No walking here."

In presentation and practice step, there are 8 activities. In Activity One, I will tell students, "Today, John is the prefect." In order to get a general meaning of the whole dialogue, students will read the question "Where are John and Tom?" firstly and listen to the dialogue from *Let's try* to get the answer. In Activity Two, some rules will be shown for students to read and choose the target rule "Quiet, please!" in a library. Next, they read the dialogue to find the target sentence "Shh, talk quietly", which has the same meaning with "Quiet, please!" In this way, a deep impression on the word "quietly" will be made from three aspects — sound, form and meaning. In Activity Four, students will look at the picture and guess what John and Tom are talking about, which means to cultivate the ability of prediction and enhance their logical thinking. Activity Five is based on group work. Firstly, students will rearrange the dialogue to get the general meaning with the help of signs. Secondly, they will underline the key sentence "Keep the desk clean" with the help of a sign so that they can link the sign with its meaning spontaneously. Activity Six is a kind of oral training by noting the rising tone , liaison , stress as well as imitating. Then a brainstorm about more rules in the library or other places such as "computer room, music room" comes off in Activity Seven. To imitate more real context, students will make a new dialogue in pairs like "Keep the … clean in/on … please. OK. I will. Thanks." What's more, students can act like either a friendly prefect or a strict one in different tones. That's funny.

Now it comes to the last step — production. It has 4 activities. First of all, students will match the pictures of uncivilized behaviors with the sentences about rules, which will stimulate their civic awareness and cultivate the problem-solving ability. Then I will ask students to listen to a chant, find the rules to get deeper impression and match the rules with signs. Next, students will watch a video, work in groups to make a new dialogue about rules in different contexts and act it out, such as in the park, on the road etc. Thus the learning difficulties of "how to lead students to apply what they have learnt to real life" will be overcome. Lastly, I will present a rhyme about rules of spring outing, and then students need to make a new rhyme in groups to check if they can use what they've learnt flexibly.

IV. Exposition

Now, please look at the blackboard. On the top, it is the title of this lesson. On the left, they are the key sentence patterns. On the right, it is the evaluation system. When students present, they can get one star like this.

As the students don't have enough time to finish the new rhyme at the end of the class, they can take it as a homework for one option. The other option is to make a new dialogue in groups and act it out. Besides, everyone will be asked to read and act out the dialogue from the book. The homework is designed at different levels, which intends to respect individual differences and protect their initiative.

V. Reflection

Generally speaking, my lesson has four outstanding merits. The first one is that I make full use of "school life" from text itself to a real life, where students get a deeper understanding of the function and meaning of the dialogue. Thus, students' output can be various. Secondly, with the help of listening to "*Let's try*", doing activities in worksheet, imitating the dialogue, students are led into the class without a hitch. Thirdly, students are the centre of the class during the whole learning process, evaluating process and homework. Last but not least, students' civic awareness is cultivated step by step through each activity. So everyone will know they are the prefects. However, how to make students talk in diverse forms is what I should think. And whether the full use of worksheet is necessary or not is a matter.

That's all for my presentation. Thanks for your listening.

（说课稿撰写者：温州市上戍小学　徐阳阳）

附：教学设计

一、教学背景

1. 教材分析

本课时选自人教版《英语》New PEP 五年级下册 Unit 6 Part B Let's talk & Let's try,单元主题是 rules,本课时教学内容为 John 和 Tom 在图书馆发生的对话。rules 这一话题是培养小学生公民意识必不可少的一块内容,所以在本课时中,学生既要学会运用主要句型... quietly. Keep your ... clean. Don't ... No, ...,并区分现在进行时和动名词的不同,同时培养小学生遵守规则的社会公共意识。

2. 学情分析

经过两年多的英语学习,小学五年级学生已经积累了一定量的关于地点名称的词汇、动词词组和表示人物性格特征的形容词,这为本课学习提供了先决条件。rules 主题与学生生活密切相关,学生有话可说,这为本课学习的话题提供了契合点。通过之前的学习,学生对于动词、校园地点名称、形容词以及科目书籍的词汇都有所积累,有助于本课的语言输出。多数学生初步具备合作意识,且自主性和逻辑能力较强,这为自主完成学习任务提供了保证。

二、 教学目标

1. 语言交际目标

(1)能理解对话大意,模仿地道的语音、语调,在具体的语境中听说认读 ... quietly, Keep your ... clean, Don't ... 和 No, ... 等句型,运用这些句型编创一个新对话并进行表演。

(2)能熟练地听说认读 Let's talk 部分对话,并在具体情境中能运用简单的英语就公共场所应注意的行为规则进行简单的询问或建议。

2. 思维认知目标

能积极和组员合作,共同完成学习单上的学习任务。积极地运用本课时所学的"Don't ..." "No, ..."等句型进行表达和交流。

3. 社会文化目标

(1)培养社会公德意识;
(2)体验因遵守公共规则而受到他人欢迎所带来的快乐。

三、 教学重难点

1. 重点:

在语境中听说认读 ... quietly, Keep your ... clean, Don't ... No, ... 等句型,区分其功能并能熟练运用。

2. 难点:

将课文对话情境进行迁移,创编新的对话。

四、 教学准备: PPT,导学单。

五、 教学过程

Step 1:Revision and lead in(9 mins)

Activity 1:Brainstorm

Review the useful words they have learned.

① T：There are many places in our school. There are many classrooms in our school. What else?

S：There is a playground.

...

② T：Look！Who are they?

S：They are students.

T：Yes. And they are prefects. Some of them are friendly. What else?

S：Some of them are ...

...

【设计说明】 激活有关学校场所的词汇和描述值日生的形容词,意在唤起旧知,为新知 rules 话题的学习做好铺垫,并创设好语言情境。

Activity 2：Group the signs

Work in groups on the worksheet：read the rules，classify them and then discuss with the group members about the regulations.

T： The prefects can tell you many rules. Here are some signs and rules. Now please take out your worksheets and read the steps first and then work in groups.

Group work 1

Steps：1. Look and read   2. Discuss and classify   3. Read and say

A Don't walk on the grass !

B No eating !

C Don't pick the flowers.

D No parking here !

E Don't climb the trees !

F Don't turn right here!

G No riding here !

H Don't write on the desk !

_____ is in/on_____.

| park | library | road |

【设计说明】 通过对导学单 Group work 1 进行反馈,呈现并板书本节课的两个重点句型 Don't ... 和 No, ... ,为下一环节这两个句型之间的相互转换做好铺垫。

Activity 3：Let's say

Transform the two sentence patterns.

120

T：Now，let's read these sentences.

S：...

T："Don't walk on the grass！" We also can say，"No walking here."
Now，can you try?

【设计说明】 通过句型转换对 Don't ... 和 No，... 进行机械操练,为学生最终能够熟练运用这两个句型打好基础。

Step 2   Presentation and practice（16 mins）

Activity 1：Listen and answer

Listen to the tape and answer the question.

T：Today，John is the prefect. He is talking with Tom. Where are they? Let's listen.

S：They are in the library.

【设计说明】 学生听录音回答问题,初步感知对话。教师借助本环节导入图书馆这一对话场景。

Activity 2：Read and say

Read the rules in the library and choose the right one that John and Tom are talking about.

T：There are many rules in the library. Let's read these rules.

S：No ... !

...

T：Which rule is John and Tom talking about?

【设计说明】 引导学生在朗读图书馆规则的过程中引出本课时的新知 Quiet，please。

Activity 3：Let's find out

Find out the expression which has the same meaning with "Quiet，please".

T：This sign means "Quiet，please". In this dialogue，which sentence has the same meaning with it?

S：Shh! Talk quietly!

【设计说明】 对话课型强调"听"的能力训练,通过听力任务的设置,让学生寻找相似句型,把词句教学中的自主权还给学生。让学生体验由 quiet 到 quietly 的词形变换,在语篇中加深对本节课的目标句型 Talk quietly 中 quietly 的音、形、义、用的理解和掌握。

Activity 4：Let's guess

Look at the picture of the dialogue carefully and guess what John and Tom are talking about.

T：Look at the picture，can you see a sign on the wall? Where are John and Tom? Can you guess? A，B or C?

A. the library   B. the books in the library   C. the rules in the library

【设计说明】 让学生结合已有的知识经验,根据 Let's talk 中的插图对文本内容进行预判,培养学生的猜测能力,提高学生的思维品质。

Activity 5：Read and order

Read and order the three parts of the dialogue，and underline the sentence according to the sign, and then practice reading in pairs.

T: They are talking about the rules in the library. Now, let's work in pairs ...

Group work 2

Steps:
1. Read and order （读对话，排序，在〇中填写正确的序号。）
2. Underline and match. （划出与标识意义相符的句子。）
3. Practise reading in groups. (同桌练习朗读对话。)

: Here they are.

: OK. Can I read the books here?

: Yes. Of course.

〇

: My name is Tom. What's your name?

: Shh.Talk quietly. I'm John.
  I can show you the English books.

: Thanks.

〇

: Anything else?

: Yes. Keep the desk clean.

: OK. I will. Thanks.

〇

【设计说明】 通过配对练习整体感知对话内容大意,并且通过看标志划句子对本课时的目标句型进行意义上的理解。

Activity 6: Imitate

Listen to the recording. Note the tone and liaison, and then imitate the dialogue.

T: Now, here are three underlined sentences. Can you listen to the tape and note the tones of the three sentences? And please note the liaison.

【设计说明】 通过听录音、标升调和连读,不仅能培养学生自主学习的能力,还能引导学生对地道的语音、语调进行模仿。

Activity 7: Think and say

Say more rules in the library and other places with the given sentence pattern "Keep ... clean".

T: Do you remember the two rules mentioned in the dialogue?

S: Talk quietly. Keep your desk clean.

T: Yes, in the library, we should keep the desk clean. And what else should Tom keep clean?

S: Keep your book clean.

S: ...

T：How about other places?

S：...

【设计说明】 在图书馆的情境中,学生结合自己的生活经验补充句子,对句型"Keep ... clean"进行操练,为 pair work 做好准备。

Activity 8：Say and act

Choose prefects with different characteristics and practice "keep ... clean" in different tones.

Say and act

Tips：A — a nice/friendly/helpful/strict/unfriendly/... prefect.

A：Keep the _____ clean in/on _____ , please.

B：OK. I will. Thanks.

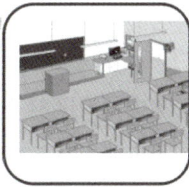

【设计说明】 学生自我管理贯穿于班级学习生活的各种不同的情境中,学生自主选择不同的值日生角色,模仿不同的语气,对句型 Keep ... clean 进行操练。

Step 3   Production（10 mins）

Activity 1：Look and match

Match the pictures with the rules on the right.

Look and match

 Keep your desk clean!

 Shh! Talk quietly!

 Shh! Work quietly!

T：We've learned some rules. Now，can you match the pictures with the sentences?

【设计说明】 图文匹配,对本节课的重点句型进行巩固,让学生通过看图听音体会这些行为的不文明之处,激发学生社会公德意识,培养学生解决问题的能力。

Activity 2：Listen and chant

Read after the tape，try to find the rules in the chant and match the rules with the signs.

T：Listen to the tape.

Ss：...

T：Let's find the rules in the chant.

Ss：...

T：There are some signs. Look! Can you match the sign with the rules?

Ss：...

Listen and chant

Let's follow the rules! Don't pick the flowers! No playing here!

Let's read the signs we see. And follow the rules，shall we?

Talk quietly，please! No running here!

Let's read the signs we see. And follow the rules，shall we?

Keep the desk clean! No eating here!

Let's read the signs we see. And follow the rules，shall we?

【设计说明】 通过歌谣回顾本课的重点句型,加深对词汇 rules 和 signs 的理解,同时在吟唱歌谣的过程中进行情感的升华,培养学生的社会公德意识。

Activity 3：Make dialogues and act out

Make a dialogue，and then act it out.

T：Now，let's enjoy a video.

S：OK.

T：Now，it's your turn to make a new dialogue in groups. Please take out the worksheets ...

Group work 3　Make a dialogue and act it out

A/B — the visitors

C/D — the prefects/the park keepers/the police

1. 小组合作讨论,确定表演场景。

2. 分角色操练对话内容,请注意正确的语音、语调并设计好动作表情。

3. 小组上台展示。

   ···

school   park   road

【设计说明】 观看短片,体验情境,小组合作创编对话并且表演,在语境中对语言进行综合运用,达到情感上的升华。

Activity 4: Make a rhyme

Make a rhyme with rules.

T: Spring is coming. Let's have a trip ... Here is a rhyme about spring outing. Discuss with your group members and make a new rhyme.

Make a new rhyme

Spring is coming.

The grass is green.

The flowers are nice.

Have a trip. To be polite.

On the road, _____.

In the park, _____.

At the zoo, _____.

Let's follow the rules, shall we?

【设计说明】 通过本课学习以及 Make a new rhyme 检测学生是否理解并能够灵活运用各种 rules,为作业环节的 Make a rhyme 做好铺垫。

六、作业布置:

	Homework	Difficulty
Required	1. Work in pairs to read and act out the dialogue in p61.	☆
Optional	2. Work in pairs to make a new dialogue about rules in classroom and act it out.	☆☆
	3. Make a new rhyme about rules.	☆☆

【设计说明】 作业 1 难度最小,是必选作业;作业 2 和作业 3 难度较大,学生可以从中选择一

个完成任务。根据难度等级设置分层作业,有利于尊重学生的个体差异,保护学生学习英语的积极性。选做作业的类型都为创编型作业,有助于培养学生的创新能力和发散思维。此外,学生合作完成作业,也有利于培养学生的合作意识。

七、板书设计:

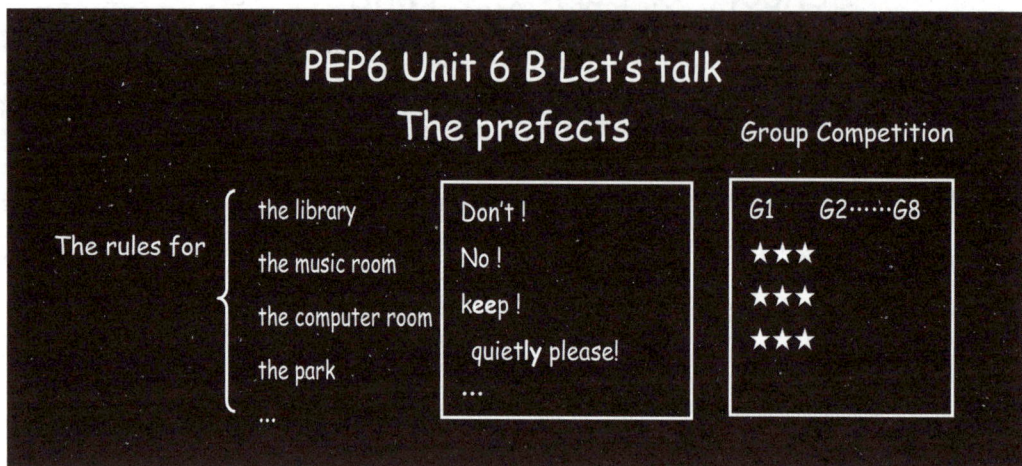

PEP6 Unit 6 B Let's talk
The prefects
Group Competition

The rules for
- the library
- the music room
- the computer room
- the park
- ...

Don't !
No !
keep !
　quietly please!
...

G1　　G2……G8
★★★
★★★
★★★

【设计说明】 板书分左右两个区域。左边区域是教学内容区域,罗列了本课以 rules 为主题的主要教学内容,即学生在 Let's talk 语言学习任务中所涉及的主要词句。右边区域是评价区域,针对导学单上的几个四人小组活动进行激励性的评价,激发学生的学习兴趣。

附:学习单

Learning Sheet for PEP 6 Unit 6 B Let's talk
The prefects

1. Pre-learning Task

1.Look and read(看标识,读句子)
2.Discuss and classify(将标识按地点分类)
3.Read and say(再读,说说你发现句型有什么规律)

A
Don't walk on the grass !

B
No eating!

C
Don't pick the flowers.

D
No parking here!

E
Don't climb the trees !

F
Don't turn right here!

G
No riding nere!

H
Don't write on the desk!

_____ in/on_____.

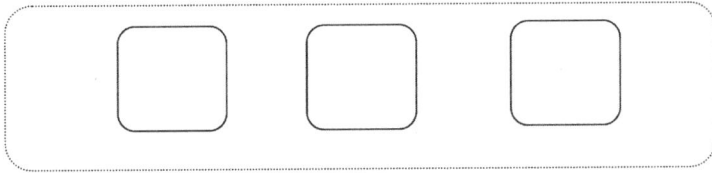

2. While-learning Task

1. Read and order （读对话，排序，在 ◯ 中填写正确的序号。）

2. Underline and match. （划出与标识意义相符的句子。）

3. Practise reading in pairs. （同桌练习朗读对话。）

4. 模仿朗读，请注意语音、语调，并标出升降调。

: <u>Here they are.</u>

: OK. <u>Can I read the books here?</u>

: Yes. Of course. ◯

: My name is Tom. What's your name?

: Shh. Talk quietly. I'm John.
   I can show you the English books. ◯

: Thanks.

: <u>Anything else?</u>

: Yes. Keep the desk clean. ◯

: OK. I will. Thanks.

3. Post-learning Task

Two visitors are in ... . What happens? Discuss and act in your group.

（两位参观者在某场所游玩或参观，他们会做些什么不文明的事情呢？两位管理员又会给他们什么建议呢？）

1. 小组合作讨论，确定表演的场景，分配角色。

2. 分角色操练对话，请注意运用正确的语音、语调和动作表情。

3. 小组上台展示。

Useful sentences(参考句型)

1. Can I _____ in/on the_____?

2. Anything else?

3. _____ quietly.

4. Keep the _____ clean.

5. No ___ing./ Don't_____.

6. _____, please.

7. Let's follow the rules, shall we?

8. OK. I will. Thanks!

...

Useful words(参考词汇)

run/jump/Sing/dance/read...

play football/...

eat hamburger/...

drink water/...

draw cartoons/...

climb the trees/...

touch the animals/...

leave rubbish(垃圾)/...

...

Homework

1.Listen and read p61.   2.Try to make a rhyme.

Spring is coming. The grass is green. The flowers are nice. Have a trip.

To be polite. On the road, _____.In the park, _____.

At the zoo, _____. Let's follow the rules, shall we?

八、 教学反思

本节课是单元的对话课,通过创设图书馆情景,运用对话模式,突出对话课型听说能力的培养。通过学习单,让孩子们在不同的场景中运用英语去挖掘和拓展教材内容。

1. 创设情境,体验习得

本课中情感态度和文化意识的体验是渗透在每个语言活动中的。其实每个学生都可以是 prefect,让孩子们在不同的场景中运用英语去体验维护社会公德而收获快乐,这也是我们挖掘和拓展教材的方向。

本课正是利用图书馆这一情境帮助学生理解有关 rules 的对话的功能和意义,从模仿开始逐步过渡到应用,并利用学生熟悉的生活场景拓展语言输出。

2. 听说领先,有效导入

本课充分运用对话内容及 Let's try 板块突出听力训练,通过听的活动导入对话教学内容,再指导他们模仿地道的语音语调,并适时渗透听力技巧,培养学生良好的交际习惯。这样长期坚持,我们会发现学生的语感提高了,口语也会有进步。

3. 自主学习,放飞课堂

本课通过学习单上 Pre-talking,While-talking 和 Post-talking 三块学生的语言活动的创设,凸显学生自主合作学习的理念,做到学习过程自主化,作业选择自主化,让学生真正成为课堂的主人。

当然,通过观摩课堂我们也看到了一些问题,如何让学生的语言活动开展得更高效,铺开的面更广,而不仅限于 pair work,group work 等形式,值得进一步探究。

(教学设计者:温州市广场路小学　刘峰)

第三部分　小学英语教研型说课案例

说课案例十一（对话课）

PEP 4 Unit 3 B Let's talk

各位老师,大家好! 我是来自温州市鞋都第一小学的黄珊瑚,刚刚为大家呈现的对话课选自人教版《英语》四年级下册第三单元 Weather 的第四课时。接下来我将从教学目标定位、教学目标达成和教学得失反思三方面和大家分享我对"小学英语对话课话题链构建"的一点理解。

微课

一、教学目标定位

首先我们谈一谈本节课的教学目标是如何定位的。本单元主题是 weather,话题为所在城市的天气情况。本课核心句型是 What's the weather like in New York/...? It's rainy/... Is it cold/...? Yes, it is. /No, it isn't。教材通过"Mark 和 Chen Jie 在电话中相互询问对方所在地的天气情况"这一对话情情,帮助学生感知上述句型的意义及语用功能,同时渗透华氏度和摄氏度的英语表达区分。对于参与本次授课的学生而言,对话难度总体不是很大。在经过一年半的英语学习之后,学生具备了一定的语言语用能力,能够较为熟练地在句型 It's ... in ... 中用 cool, cold, hot, warm 等形容词描述各地的天气,同时对温度和相应气候表述都有一定的知识储备。此外,班级学生活泼好动,思维比较活跃,具有较强的好奇心和表现欲,因此,在教学过程的设计中,我设置了一些需要学生动脑思考的、开放性问题和学习任务,减少机械操练,增加学生自主表达的机会。

基于上述教材梳理和学情分析,我设置了以下的教学目标,下面将从语言交际目标、思维认知目标和社会文化目标这三个维度来进行陈述。

1. 语言交际目标

(1) 在语境中了解 5 个城市(New York, Sydney, Toronto, Beijing, London),理解 rainy, degree 的意思并能正确运用;

(2) 理解对话大意并在一定情境中运用句型 What's the weather like in New York/...? It's rainy/... 来询问某地天气情况;能运用句型 Is it cold/...? Yes, it is. /No, it isn't 来确认某地天气状况,并运用句型 It's ... degrees 来描述气温。

(3) 按照意群朗读对话,做到语音、语调正确。

2. 思维认知目标

（1）借助话题链，使学生能够在具体的语境中主动提问，提升思维品质。

（2）通过小组合作，完成天气报告的任务，提高语言运用的交流与协作能力。

3. 社会文化目标

了解中西方对气温描述的差异，掌握温度的两种读法（℃ 和℉）；能够根据世界重要城市的天气情况，运用核心句型用英语谈论各地城市天气情况，互相交流天气信息。

二、 教学目标达成

经过一节课的学习，我认为本节课的教学目标初步达成，接下来将重点说说本节课教学目标是如何达成的。

首先是语言交际目标。在本课教学中，通过 weather 这个主话题，教师创设了 3 个子话题，先和学生聊聊自己所在的城市天气，再过渡到课文 Mark 和 Chen Jie 所在的城市天气，最后通过 May Day 的衔接过渡到学生放假要去的旅游城市的天气情况。通过这 3 个不同情境的创设，不断复现核心语言，在新的话题情境中巩固核心语言，帮助学生提升语用能力，尤其是在话题 3 的语言输出中，学生参与积极，语言交际十分完整有效。

在第二个子话题中出现了本课的教学难点，即学生无法理解课文中 Mark 所说的 26 degrees. That's cold。因此，在该环节的处理中，我先让学生通过自身知识积累去判断 26 degrees. It's warm. 是否正确；然后组织小组讨论，为什么 Mark 认为"26 degrees. That's cold"；再通过微课，直观展示华氏度和摄氏度的区分，同时在视频中滚动复现本课第二组核心句型 Is it...? Yes, it is. /No, it isn't。最后，通过两个 Tasks 的练习，检查学生的理解与掌握情况。应该说，通过这一系列的活动，学生能够理解华氏和摄氏的表达区别，同时也能运用华氏度、摄氏度完成话题 3 的语言交际任务。当然，最后我们还是要回归文本，关注学生的文本朗读能力。通过听音标升降调和跟读、齐读课文等活动多层次、多角度地认读课文，重复听音，听说结合，注重语音、语调，有效培养学生的听读和朗读能力。

此外，在思维认知目标上，教师应不断关注学生的"问"。只有学生有疑问，他们才会去关注答案，才能有思维上的训练。在本堂课教学中，我尽量通过不同的形式勾起学生的好奇心，调动他们的积极性。在子话题 1 中，因为大家同处一地，如果让生生互问对方所在地天气是无效也无意义的。这个时候教师出示温州各地的地图，同时隐藏气象图标，引导学生问 What's the weather like in____，而教师扮演的天气预报员，每出现一个图标说一次：It's rainy，让无趣的答句变得生动，学生好奇我的下一个答句，也好奇下一个地方的天气情况，自然就更愿意举手去问，去发言。

同样，在子话题 2 中，我设计了 3 个小任务：Listen and answer, Look and say 和 Watch and answer，让学生带着问题去听、去看，找到 Mark 的所在地以及当地的天气状况，还有 Chen Jie 所在的 Beijing 的温度，然后利用核心句型 What's the weather like in... 来进行问答。如此一来，学生所做的每一步都有他的方向性和目标性,每一步都是在验证自己心中的答案。

最后,在子话题 3 中,教师通过教材续编,创设了"Mark 之所以打电话给 Chen Jie,是因为自己五一放假要来北京看长城"这一完整的故事情节。随着教学步骤的推进,教师进一步走向学生生活实际,询问学生:你们五一放假要去哪儿呢? 那边的天气是怎么样的? 同时出示这个黑板上的表格,进行小组问答。学生除了要完成自己的出行安排及相关的天气说明,还要记录同伴的相关信息。这样一来,学生要想完成表格,就一定要张嘴去问他的小伙伴,这个时候板书上的句型就自然而然地被使用,语言的输出真实有效。在这一整节课的教学中,通过这一系列的提问,学生的思维一直在运转,他们获取的信息都是他们自己思考后的成果,应该说本课的认知思维目标还是初步达成的。

另外,在子话题 3 中,学生根据教师所给的各地天气预报安排自己的出行计划并询问他人的假期安排。在该活动中,学生需要清楚中西方的气温表达差异,确定自己想要去的城市,同时运用本课的核心句型和小伙伴相互交流各自的假期安排。从最后的展示环节,我们可以清晰地看到学生表达自然,沟通流畅,很好地达成了本课的教学目标。

三、 教学得失反思

接下来,我来反思一下本节课的教学亮点和存在的问题。本课教学中,我始终贯彻以学生为中心、循序渐进的教学原则。从本课导入环节到 3 个子话题的延伸拓展,整体教学思路清晰,班级课堂学生发言活跃,活动积极。本节课的成功之处有以下几点:

1. 主线明确,话题贯通

对话语篇教学,教师首先要关注的就是我们到底可以和学生聊什么。本课中本人构建了 3 个基于 weather 的子话题,通过不断深入对话,从易到难,层层递进,让学生在真实的语言环境中轻松、愉悦地对 weather 这一话题进行不断讨论。整节课通过话题链的上下连接,使师生之间的对话更加自然真实,充分实现了对话教学的最终目的,即运用所学语言进行相关话题的交际。

2. 问题驱动,思维在线

提问是探究的前提,学生提问能力是科学素养形成的必要因素之一。只有当学生好奇"为什么""怎么了""是我想的这样子吗"的时候,思维才算是真正启动,因为学生能自主提问才能有效促进其思维发展。在本课教学中,因为学生自己所在的学校在下雨,所以好奇温州其他各地的天气情况,从而有了话题 1 Wenzhou's weather;因为大家在讨论表达对 rainy day 的喜好从而认识了新朋友 Mark,所以有了话题 2 New York's weather,开始好奇为什么 Mark 所说的 26 degrees 和自己所理解的不一样;从 Mark"五一"的出行计划联想到自己,开始好奇小伙伴的假期出行安排,所以出现了话题 3 Other cities' weather。就这样,3 个子话题的开展都是基于学生"问"的前提,学生不断地产生疑问,验证疑问,回答疑问。如此一来,学生不是被动地接受教师提问,而是主动提问,为了知道自己想要的答案而去学习,这个时候的学习才算是真正意义上的思维在线,自主学习。

3. 微课辅助,难点突破

本课的文化学习目标是通过本课学习,学生能明白不同国家所用的温度计量单位是不一样的。然而,在日常教学中,如何让学生明白这两个计量单位的不同,往往需要大量的语言讲解,费时费力,学生最后依然是一知半解。微课的使用可以让学生更加直观清晰地明了教材中摄氏度和华氏度的知识点。教学时无需多言,学生都能做到心中有数。

当然,本节课还有很多不尽如人意的地方:如教师用语还不够精简明确,对后 20% 学生的关注度还不够全面,等等,这些都需要在之后的课堂里进一步改正。

以上就是我对"小学英语对话课话题链构建"的一些理解和尝试,希望大家多提宝贵建议。

(说课稿撰写者:温州市鞋都第一小学 黄珊瑚)

附:教学设计

一、 教学背景

1. 教材分析

本课为人教版《英语》四年级下册第三单元的第四课时,是一节对话教学课。本单元主题是"weather",话题为所在城市天气状况。本课核心句型是 What's the weather like in New York/…? It's rainy/… 及 Is it cold/…? Yes, it is. /No, it isn't. 教材通过 Chen Jie 和 Mark 在电话中相互询问所在地天气情况这一对话情景,帮助学生在对话情景中感知上述句型的意义和语用功能,并区分华氏度和摄氏度的表达。

2. 学情分析

本节课的授课对象是小学四年级学生,他们能够较为熟练地在句型 It's … in … 中用 cool, cold, hot, warm 等形容词描述各地的天气,同时对温度和相应气候的表述都有一定的知识储备。此外,他们思维活跃、活泼好动,具有较强的好奇心和表现欲,故而在教学过程的设计中,教师要多设置一些需要动脑思考、开放性的问题和学习任务,减少机械操练,增加学生自主表达的机会。

二、 教学目标

1. 语言交际目标

(1)在语境中了解 5 个城市(New York, Sydney, Toronto, Beijing, London)及理解

rainy，degree 的意思并能正确运用。

（2）理解对话大意并在一定情境中运用句型 What's the weather like in New York/...？It's rainy/... 来询问某地天气情况；能运用句型 Is it cold/...？Yes，it is. /No，it isn't 来确认某地天气状况，并运用句型 It's ... degrees 来描述气温。

（3）按照意群朗读对话，做到语音、语调正确。

2. 思维认知目标

通过话题链的创设，学生能够提升"主动提问"的能力，增强用英语询问他人天气的自信心并主动使用英语表达自己的兴趣。

3. 社会文化目标

了解中西方对气温描述的差异，掌握温度的两种读法（℃ 和 ℉），能够根据世界重要城市的天气情况，运用核心句型用英语谈论各地城市天气情况，互相交流天气信息。

三、 教学重难点

1. 教学重点

掌握和运用句型 What's the weather like in New York/...？It's rainy/... 及 Is it cold/...？Yes，it is. /No，it isn't.

2. 教学难点

正确区分温度的两种读法（℃和℉）及其描述差异；结合一些城市的天气情况，运用核心句型来完成对话。

四、 教学准备

多媒体课件、微课视频、希沃一体机、平板电脑（教师用）、学习单。

五、 教学准备

Step 1　Warming-up & revision (5 mins)

Activity 1：Sing songs

A. Sing a song：*Weather song*.

Students sing after teacher，and then teacher uses the screen shot of the song.

T：What's the weather like in this picture?

Ss：It's rainy.

T：Yes，we can see much rain in the sky，so it's rainy now. Please read after me：What's the weather like?

Ss：What's the weather like? (for 3 times)

B. Sing the second song：What's the weather like?

Weather Song

It's rainy day today, rainy day, rainy day,

It's rainy day today, wet, wet, wet.

It's sunny day today, sunny day, sunny day,

It's sunny day today, hot, hot, hot.

It's cloudy day today, cloudy day, cloudy day,

It's cloudy day today, warm, warm, warm.

It's windy day today, windy day, windy day,

It's windy day today, cool, cool, cool.

It's snowy day today, snowy day, snowy day,

It's snowy day today, cold, cold, cold.

What's the weather like?

What's the weather like?

What's the weather like?

What's the weather like today?

What's the weather like?

What's the weather like?

What's the weather like today?

It's rainy. It's cloudy.

It's windy.

And it's snowy.

【设计说明】 通过吟唱,初步认识描述天气的单词,同时师生间良好的互动营造了轻松的英语学习氛围。此外,第二首歌曲滚动复现句型:What's the weather like? 完成大量听的输入和唱的输出。同时,教师引导学生理解 rain—rainy 的词性变化,为后续学习有关天气的单词做铺垫。

Step 2   Wenzhou's weather (4 mins)

Answer what the weather is like in different places in Wenzhou with a weather map.

T:(Points to the outside.) What's the weather like today?

Ss:It's rainy.

T:Yes,it's rainy outside. How about other places in Wenzhou?

(Teacher shows a weather forecast map in Wenzhou covering the weather icons)

T:Look,here's a map of Wenzhou. What do you want to know?

S1:What's the weather like in _____?

T:It's rainy.

S2：What's the weather like in _____?

T：...

【设计说明】 因上课时节正值雨季,温州各地都在下雨,如果让生生互问,则会显得较为机械、无趣。而地图的隐藏图标让学生好奇,而教师扮演的天气预报员出示一个图标说一次 It's rainy,让无趣的答句变得尤为生动,学生更愿意去说去问,同时也为下一环节的对话活动做好了铺垫。

Step 3　The weather in New York (15 mins)

Activity 1：Listen, look and answer

Teacher will introduce several new friends to students, and lead students to talk about the weather in their cities.

T：(Shows the whole map) Oh, no! It's rainy everywhere. Do you like rainy day?

Ss：Yes/No.

T：It's OK. Different people have different outlooks on rainy day. Here comes a boy who doesn't like rainy day. Can you read his name?

Ss：M-ar-k, Mark.

T：Do you know Mark? What do you want to know?

S1：Who is Mark?

S2：How old is Mark?

S3：Where is Mark?

T：(Guides students to watch illustrations.) Look, Mark is talking on the phone. Do you know whom Mark is talking with?

Ss：...

T：(Shows the second picture.) Mark is talking with Chen Jie. So, Mark is Chen Jie's friend. Can you guess, where is Mark?

Ss：...

T：Now let's listen and answer：Where is Mark?

(Students listen to the recording of the conversation for the first time with their predictions, and then check the answers.)

T：OK. Question 2. Who can read it for us?

S1：What's the weather like in New York?

T：Good! So what's the weather like in New York?

Ss：It's rainy.

T：Yes, from the dialogue and this picture, we can know it's rainy in New York. How about Chen Jie? Where is Chen Jie?

Ss：Beijing.

T：What's the weather like in Beijing?

Ss：...

T：OK，this time，let's watch and answer：What's the temperature in Beijing?

(Teacher presents a thermometer to guide the students to know the key word of the question is "temperature".)

【设计说明】　整体语言教学理念下的对话教学主张教师整体导入文本,引导学生整体理解语篇,同时在对话教学中引导学生进行自主观察和预测。大部分学生在完成第一次听的练习后,其实对第二个问题已有答案。这时候我们要关注后20％的学生,引导学生在听的同时借助插图理解对话大意。三个问题的解决关联着三次文本的听和理解,通过试听结合、回答问题的形式学生进一步从整体上理解、感知课文。此外,在做听力的同时,教师要重视对学生听力策略的训练,培养学生听前阅读题干、抓关键信息的能力,以确保听力训练的有效性。

Activity 2：Good to know

Learn the difference between Fahrenheit and Celsius.

T：It's 26 degrees in Beijing. Is it cold? Is it hot? Is it warm?

Ss：Yes/No.

T：Why does Mark say，"26 degrees! That's cold?" Please discuss in your group.

Ss：... (Discuss and say)

T：Chen Jie is talking about degree Centigrade，but Mark is talking about degree Fahrenheit. They are different. 26 degrees Fahrenheit is ...

Ss：Cold.

(Students watch a video about Celsius and Fahrenheit. After watching，they complete the first task exercise on the task list.)

Read and match			
13℃	warm	<50°F cold	<10℃ cold
47°F	cool	50 – 68°F cool	10 – 20℃ cool
35℃	hot	68 – 82°F warm	20 – 28℃ warm
70°F	cold	>82°F hot	>28℃ hot

【设计说明】　在该环节中,学生需要观察课文插图,理解对话大意,同时具有一定课外知识基础,才会发现华氏和摄氏的区别。此外,通过微课直观展示华氏度和摄氏度的区别,同时在视频中滚动复现本课句型 Is it ...? Yes/No. 在该环节中教师要注重培养学生的思维品质,提高学生的逻辑思维能力,同时培养学生与同伴交流的意识。

Activity 3：Let's talk

Talk about the weather in different cities.

T：Look here! It is 15 degrees in Beijing. Is it cold in Beijing?

S：No!

T：Yes，from this chart，we know 15 degrees Centigrade is cool，so we can answer："No，it isn't. It's cool in Beijing." (Teacher gives an example.)

Ss：(Repeat.)

T：Here is something about other cities. Let's have a look.

(Students learn the names of cities：New York，London，Sydney，Toronto.)

According to the chart，students choose a city and make a dialogue to complete the second task on the worksheet.

Let's talk

New York (68℉)　　　　Sydney (86℉)

London (41℉)

Toronto (45℉)　　　　Beijing (15℃)

A：Is it _____ in _____?

B：Yes, it is.

/No, it isn't. it's _____.

(hot/warm/cold/cool)

【设计说明】 学生根据教师所给的城市信息进行对话操练,在这个环节中,我们不仅要关注学生核心语言的应用,还要提升学生的思维品质。

Activity 4：Let's wrap it up

Listen to the recording and imitate it，and pay attention to the tones and sentence stresses.

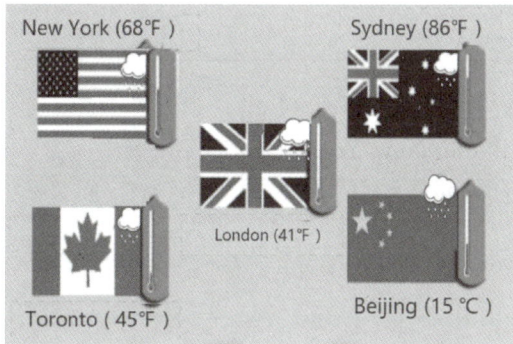

Let's talk

Hi, Chen Jie! This is Mark.

Hi, Mark! What's the weather like in New York?

It's rainy. How about Beijing? Is it cold?

请校对一下你作的标注是否正确。

再读一次课文，注意语音语调。

No, it isn't. It's 26 degrees.

26 degrees! That's cold!

Huh? No, it's not. It's warm!

【设计说明】 学生根据录音内容,标注升降调,再校对并读一读自己已校对正确的文本,最后进行模仿朗读和分角色对话。多层次、多角度地跟读课文,重复听音,听说有机结合,注重语音、语调,有效培养学生的听说能力。

Step 4　Other cities' weather (11 mins)

Activity 1：Plan the travel

A. Lead in.

Know Mark's travel plan on May Day.

T：Why does Mark make a call to Chen Jie?

S：... (Guess)

T：Maybe. Let's have a look.

(Students read the whole dialogue.)

Mark：Hi, Chen Jie. This is Mark.

Chen Jie：Hi, Mark. What's the weather like in New York?

Mark：It's rainy. How about Beijing? Is it cold?

Chen Jie：No, it isn't. It's 26 degrees.

Mark：26 degrees! That's cold!

Chen Jie：Huh? No, it's not. It's warm!

Mark：Warm? Great! I'm going to Beijing on May Day!

Chen Jie：Really? Welcome!

T：May Day is coming, so Mark is going to ...

Ss：Beijing.

【设计说明】 有时出于篇幅的限制或核心句型要求,教材中的文本往往只能呈现话题情境的一小部分。这个时候教师从生活实际出发,延续教材对话,对教材语境进行整合和补充,把话题导入到新的情境中,如"五一"劳动节,以帮助学生丰富语言输出,让学生在新的语言形式中灵活运用所学知识。

B. Talk about travel plans.

Talk about their travel plans for May Day with Teacher.

T：Where are you going on May Day? For me，I'm going to Sanya. How about you?

S1：I'm going to ...

S2：...

T：You have a lot of travel plans. You know we should get things ready before we depart，right? First, we should know the weather there，right?

S：Yes.

T：Here are weather reports of some cities on May Day. Look here, this is Sanya. It's 32 degrees. It's hot. So, this is my plan.

(Teacher fills in the table on the blackboard and say：Mark is going to Beijing. It's 26 degrees. It's warm. And I'm going to Sanya. It's 32 degrees. It's hot.)

Name	City	℃/℉	Weather
Mark	Beijing	26℃	warm
Miss Huang	Sanya	32℃	hot

T：Where are you going? Please choose one place that you want to go on May Day and fill in the table.

The weather report for the 'most popular' city on May day
（五一出行"最热门"城市／国家天气预报）

Sanya	32℃	New York	68℉
Shanghai	22℃	Sydney	86℉
Chengdu	18℃	London	62℉
Kunming	28℃	Toronto	59℉
Guangzhou	23℃	Singapore	82℉
Shenzhen	30℃	Canada	59℉
Chongqing	19℃	Korea	24℃
Xi'an	13℃	Japan	18℃
Hangzhou	22℃	Thailand	34℃
Xiamen	24℃		

(Students fill in the table on their worksheet and say：I'm going to _____. It's _____ degrees. It's _____.)

【设计说明】 在真实的语言环境中,学生更加有话可说,跃跃欲试。该表格的填写和输出可以帮助学生更清晰地明确自己的出行计划,同时为后续的对话做好铺垫。

C. Fill in the table.

Teacher asks a student to complete the third row of the above table.

T：Hello，_____. Where are you going?

S：I am going to_____.

T：What's the weather like in _____?

S：It's_____ degrees. It's _____.

(PPT shows the conversation A.)

Teacher asks another student to show the other dialogue，and complete the fourth row of the above table.

T：Hey，_____! Where are you going?

S：I'm going to _____.

T：What's the weather like in _____?

S：It's_____ degrees. It's _____.

T：How about _____? My mom is going to _____. Is it _____?

S：Yes，it is. It's _____ degrees.

/No，it isn't. It's _____ degrees. It's _____.

(PPT shows the conversation B.)

D. Talk about travel plans in groups.

Students ask and complete the form on the worksheet in their own group（choose Conversation A or B），then present the dialogues.

【设计说明】 该环节涵盖本课所有的核心句子与教学难点,要求学生在掌握语言技能的同时要有逻辑思维判断的能力(℃和℉的区分)。同时在学生展示对话前,教师提出问题: Where does he/she want to go? What's the weather like there? 让其他同学带着问题去听,再一次训练学生听的能力,同时集中学生注意力,让语用的输入、输出都变得及时有效。此外,教师应及时给予评价,包括表演者及认真聆听的同学,以调动学生积极性。

Activity 2：Let's find

Find out the transformation rule of weather words.

T：This is a picture on your worksheet，and this is on your book. Can you find any difference?

Ss：... （In Chinese)

T：Yes! We see the rain. It's rainy. We see the cloud. It's cloudy. Please find the other weather words after class. It's your homework.

Let's find

请找找剩下3幅图片中的气候单词变化规律，可参考p28

cloud ⟶ cloudy

rain ⟶ rainy

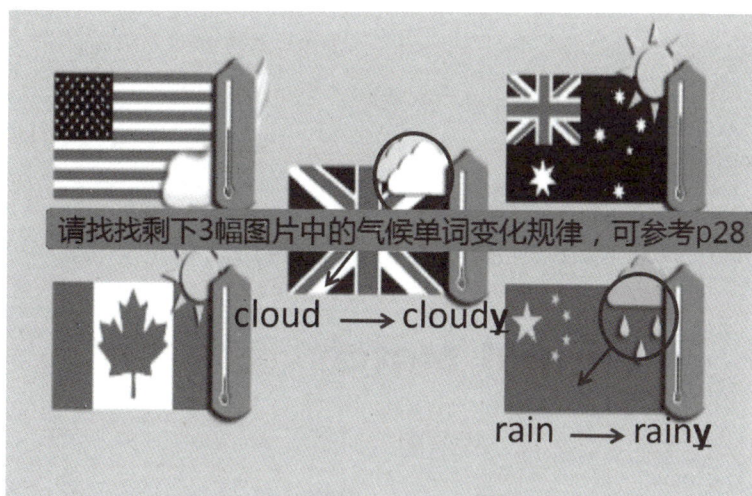

【设计说明】 通过本课 rain−rainy 的学习,学生能够理解天气单词的变化规律,为下一课时的 Let's learn 教学做好铺垫。

六、 作业布置

1. Listen to the recording and read the dialogue on p27.
2. Find out the transformation rule of weather words for the remaining 3 pictures of p27 and try to read it. (Reference P28)

【设计说明】 作业 1 属常规作业,听读课文,目的是夯实基础;作业 2 是预习作业,将 p27 的 Let's play 和 p28 的新课联系在一起,学生发现、探索并得出结论,为下一课的新知学习做好预热。

七、 板书设计

weather

---PEP 4 Unit 3 B Let's talk

A: Where are you going?
B: I'm going to Beijing.
A: What's the weather like in Beijing?
B: It's 26 degrees. It's warm.
A: How about Sanya? I'm going to Sanya.
Is it cold?
B: Yes, it is. It's _____ degrees.
/No, it isn't. It's 32 degrees. It's hot.

Name	City	Weather	℃/℉
Mark	Beijing	warm	26℃
Miss Huang	Sanya	hot	32℃

附: 学习单

一、**Read and match.**（看图,连线。注意图表的使用）

Read and match

13°C	warm
47°F	cool
35°C	hot
70°F	cold

<50°F	cold		<10°C	cold
50-68°F	cool		10-20°C	cool
68-82°F	warm		20-28°C	warm
>82°F	hot		>28°C	hot

二、**Let's talk.**（请任选图片中某一个城市和同桌完成对话,可参考第一题图表）

New York (68°F)

Sydney (86°F)

London (41°F)

Toronto (45°F)

Beijing (15 °C)

A：Is it ____ in ____?

B：Yes, it is.

/No, it isn't. It's ____.

三、**Fill and say.**（完成表格，并选择相应文本完成对话）

1. 安排自己的假期并填入表格第一行，再说一说：

Name	City	℃ / ℉	Weather

I'm going to _____. It's _____ degrees. It's _____.

2. 选择 A/B 对话，完成表格第二行（可多询问几个小伙伴，记录在学习单背面）。

(A)

A：Where are you going?

B：I'm going to ____.

A：What's the weather like in ____?

B：It's ____ degrees. It's ____.

(B)

A：Where are you going?

B：I'm going to____.

A：What's the weather like in____?

B：It's ____ degrees. It's____.

A：How about ____? I'm going to ____.

　　Is it ____?

B：Yes, it is. It's ____ degrees.

　　/No, it isn't. It's ____ degrees. It's____.

八、教学反思

　　本课教学中，教师始终贯彻以学生为中心、循序渐进的教学原则，从本课导入环节到 3 个子话题的延伸拓展，整体思路清晰，教学环节顺畅有序，较好地实现了本课教学目标。当然，本次教学设计也有一些不足之处：如教师用语还不够精简明确，对后 20％学生的关注不够等，这些都需要在以后的教学中进一步改进（具体分析可参见前文内容）。

（教学设计者：温州市鞋都第一小学　黄珊瑚）

PEP 2 Unit 4 Where is my car? B Start to read

各位老师好，刚刚给大家呈现的阅读课选自人教版《英语》三年级下册第四单元 *Where is my car?* 的第六课时，是一节启蒙阅读课。接下来我将从教学目标定位、教学目标达成和教学得失反思三方面与大家分享我对小学英语阅读启蒙课的思考。

一、 教学目标定位

我先来谈一下我是如何定位这节课的教学目标的。本单元的话题是物品的位置，核心句型为 Where is Zip? Is it in/on/under ...? Yes, it is. /No, it isn't. 重点词汇主要有 desk，chair，toy，boat，box，ball，bear 等，虽然之前学过这些内容，但是一部分学生掌握得不够好，因此需要教师复习旧知，同时鼓励学生运用阅读技巧，如看图预测、捕捉关键信息，从而完成一个有意义的语篇综合性训练活动。我们班的学生刚刚接触英语半年，词汇积累和知识储备非常有限，因此阅读能力较弱，需要教师的引导。但作为三年级的学生，他们有较强的好奇心，具有好活动、爱表现、善模仿的心理特点，因此小组活动和模仿朗读等教学活动比较容易开展且能取得较好效果。基于上述教材梳理和学情分析，我制定了语言交际目标、思维认知目标和社会文化目标。

1. 语言交际目标

（1）能在真实的语境中，运用核心语言询问和猜测物品位置并回答。

（2）能在图片和教师的帮助下认读句子，并利用这些句子回答 Zoom 提出的问题，找到 Zip 的位置。

（3）能在阅读文本时，运用升调来朗读一般疑问句。

2. 思维认知目标

（1）能通过图文配对，提高认读理解能力，通过看图，预测位置，提升推理分析能力。

（2）能通过对话编创和同伴共同完成角色扮演任务，提高语言运用层次的认知能力。

3. 社会文化目标

能意识到要养成整理书包的良好学习习惯。

二、 教学目标达成

接着我们来回顾一下本节课的教学目标是如何通过相应的教学活动——达成的。本节课可以分为热身、读前、读中和读后四个环节。

在课堂一开始,教师带领学生一起唱歌、做游戏,调动了课堂的气氛,也复习了这单元的核心词汇和句型。学生对 In,On,Under 这首歌比较熟悉,因此他们可以一边唱歌一边做动作,快速进入学习状态。"打羽毛球"游戏也是教师和学生在课上进行互动的方式,所以该游戏可以让学生都能够积极地参与进来。在接下来的活动中,学生能够在图片的帮助下,运用重点词汇和句型成功地找到玩具熊的位置。在这些活动过程中,学生不仅巩固了本单元的一些重点单词和句型,而且他们对这节课的兴趣和热情也被激发了出来。

在"读前"环节,我设计了两个活动。首先,我自己设计了一个 Zoom 和 Zip 之间的对话,对话主要讲述了 Zoom 正在整理书包去上学,但是找不到自己的书本。在 Zip 的帮助下,他找到了书本。对话的内容贴近学生实际生活,互动效果好,在师生模拟对话时,学生掌握了对话的基本结构。在接下来的同伴合作对话环节中,学生根据自己的能力选择了不同难度的任务。虽然情景与上面师生对话相似,但学生们可以自己进行思考,新编对话,进行角色扮演。学生能在真实的语境中,运用核心语言询问和猜测物品位置并回答,第一个语言交际目标达成。

在前面的基础上,我又呈现了课文中的情境,学生通过看图,以及关注图中的"足迹"来预测 Where is Zip? 前面的活动已经为这个环节的开展做好了铺垫,所以可以看到大部分学生都能够积极参与到和教师的互动中来。

我在读中环节共设计了 4 个活动来促成教学目标的达成。一开始图文配对培养了学生认读的能力。接下来的细读文本并划出含有 in/on/under 的介词短语的活动也为下一个环节——确认 Zip 的位置做了铺垫。为了确认 Zip 的位置,学生需要静下心来,再次仔细地去阅读文本。在这个过程中,第二个语言交际目标达成。这还能体现出教师对学生阅读技巧的锻炼,如借助关键词来寻找信息。而事实也证明,他们能够在教师的引导下,更好地运用阅读技巧以提升捕捉信息的能力,基本上大部分学生都能够准确地找到 Zip 的位置。除此之外,教师还应注重对学生正确语音语调的锻炼和培养,因此,在本课中设计了模仿阅读活动。当教师播放音频的时候,学生都会自觉地跟着录音朗读阅读材料,这与我对他们平时习惯的培养是分不开的。其次在这篇阅读材料中,学生需要重点关注一般疑问句的升调处理,所以我特地播放了两次录音,让学生自己去发现一般疑问句的结尾要读升调。事实上,学生也的确发现了这种规律,所以学生第二遍跟着录音读的时候,会有意识地去读升调,达成第三个语言交际目标。为了练习和巩固学生的语音、语调,我又设计了小组合作模仿朗读文本的活动。大家可以看到,小组成员为了让小组朗读呈现的效果更好,小组成员间会相互监督,发现和纠正同伴出现的问题,而且一些表现较好的学生能够积极帮助一些基础较弱的伙伴,告诉他们要如何改进。

最后的"读后"环节一共设计了两个活动。首先,我设计了一个新的情境对话,以 careless John 为主题,包含 John,Amy,Sara 三个人物。和前面新情境的导入类似,我依旧采用了图片导入的形式,当我问 Where is John's ruler? 时,我先让学生通过看图来猜测 Is it on the desk? Is it on the book? 等,然后再阅读文本确认他们的猜测,培养学生推理层次的认知能力,第一个思维认知目标得以达成。我们可以发现,学生能够在接下来的角色扮演环节中还原对话的情境。之后,我还设置了小组合作对话活动,学生可以自己进行思考,新编对话,并且非常出色地进行角色扮演。这个过程培养了语用层次的认知能力,第二个思维认知目标顺利达成。学生不仅巩固了这节课所学习的内容,还意识到了自己在生活中要养成整理书包的好习惯,社会文化目标达成,同时,学生的合作能力也进一步得到了提升。

三、 教学得失反思

最后,我来反思一下本节课的教学亮点和存在的问题。本节课属于小学低年级学段阅读启蒙课。我以本课的话题"寻找物品"为主线,一方面复习了本单元的核心句型,如 Where is Zip? Is it in/on/under ...? Yes, it is. /No, it isn't. 另一方面培养了学生的阅读技巧,如看图预测、捕捉关键信息。本节课的亮点可以从以下几个方面来说:

1. 层层推进,提升学生思维品质

在本节课中,我非常关注我们班学生思维品质的提升。首先,图文配对活动培养学生认读理解能力。其次,看图预测位置的活动让学生进行思考推理来做出自己的猜测,提升推理分析能力。最后,我还给学生机会去创编对话,完成角色扮演,促进其语用能力的提高。从理解到推理再到语用,层层推进,逐步提高学生的认知能力,提升学生的思维品质。

2. 步步为营,培养学生阅读策略

我们班学生接触英语阅读的时间较短,阅读能力较弱,所以我在课堂上设计了一系列活动,来帮助学生理解文本,一步步培养他们的阅读策略。首先,在略读标序号的活动中,学生阅读文本圈出关于"位置"的单词,并在图片上标序号,进行图文配对。接着,我又设计了细读文本,带领学生划出关键信息的活动。学生在这一活动中关注 in/on/under 这些方位介词来获取关键信息。最后,学生能够根据前两步的铺垫,通过精读句子正确地做出判断。

3. 合作学习,提高学生课堂参与度

我在同伴合作活动中采用分层任务设计的方式,鼓励每个学生都参与到课堂活动中,皆有表现自我的机会;在文本朗读环节采用小组合作模仿朗读文本的形式,帮助学习能力相对较弱的学生运用正确的语音语调朗读文本,引导每个学生都能积极参与学习活动。

本节课也存在一些不足的地方,比如我的指令语有时不够精简概括,对学生的评价也存在不够具体的情况等,需要在今后的教学中不断改进。当然,还会有其他不足之处,希望各位同仁提出宝贵的建议,谢谢大家!

(说课稿撰写者:浙江师范大学外国语学院　陈梦婷)

PEP 2 Unit 4 Where is my car? B Start to read

一、教学背景

1. 教材分析

本课选自人教版《英语》三年级下册第四单元 *Where is my car?* 的第六课时，是一节阅读启蒙教学课。本单元的话题是物品的位置。该话题知识与学生生活紧密联系。本课时通过寻找 Zip 给学生提供了一个有一定意义的语篇综合性的训练活动，帮助学生进一步巩固本单元的核心词汇和句型。

本单元的核心句型有 Where is Zip? Is it in/on/under … ? Yes, it is. /No, it isn't. 教材通过寻找 Zip 这一情景，进一步运用核心单词和句型，同时训练学生的阅读技巧，如看图预测、捕捉关键信息等。

2. 学情分析

本节课的学习对象是小学三年级学生，他们刚刚接触英语半年，词汇积累和知识储备非常有限，阅读能力较弱，需要教师的引导。但是他们具有好奇心、好活动、爱表现、善模仿等特点，乐于参加小组合作，对英语学习充满兴趣。学生在本单元前几节课中已经学习了核心句型 Where is Zip? Is it in/on/under … ? Yes, it is. /No, it isn't 和重点词汇 desk, chair, toy, boat, box, ball, bear 等，但是有一部分学生掌握得还不够好，需要进一步练习和巩固。

二、教学目标

1. 语言交际目标

（1）能在真实的语境中，运用核心语句询问和猜测物品位置并回答。

（2）能在图片和教师的帮助下认读句子，并利用这些句子回答 Zoom 提出的问题，找到 Zip 的位置。

（3）能在阅读文本时，运用升调来朗读一般疑问句。

2. 思维认知目标

（1）能通过图文配对，提高认读理解能力，通过看图，预测位置，提升推理分析能力。

（2）能通过对话编创和同伴共同完成角色扮演任务，达成语言运用层次的认知能力。

3. 社会文化目标

能意识到要养成整理书包的良好学习习惯。

三、教学重难点

1. 教学重点

在图片和教师的帮助下认读句子,并利用这些句子回答 Zoom 提出的问题,找到 Zip 的位置。

2. 教学难点

在真实的语境中,运用核心语句进行对话创编,询问和猜测物品位置并回答。

四、教学准备

多媒体课件、单词条、学习单。

五、教学过程

Step 1　Revision and warming-up (5 mins)

Activity 1：Sing and act

Sing the song *On*，*in*，*under* and do the actions.

Lyrics

On，in，under

On，in，under，clap，clap，clap.

On，in，under，clap，clap，clap.

On，in，under，clap，clap，clap.

On my cars，in my cars，under my cars

On in under，clap，clap，clap.

...

【设计说明】　课前唱歌做动作,呈现课堂话题,活跃课堂气氛,带领学生迅速进入英语学习状态。

Activity 2：Play badminton

Do the action like playing badminton and read aloud the words.

T：Let's play badminton together. Read the words aloud. （T shows some pictures and presents the words, such as desk, chair, toy, boat，box，ball，bear and so on.）

S：...

(Pay attention to the last word "bear", and know it is a toy bear "Zoom".)

【设计说明】　通过"打羽毛球"的游戏,复习单元核心词汇。

Activity 3：Let's guess

Look at the pictures and guess where the toy bear is. Students can guess "Is it in/on/ under . . . ?"

T：Oh, it's a toy bear. Now it hides in one place. Now where is it? Can you find it? Let's guess!

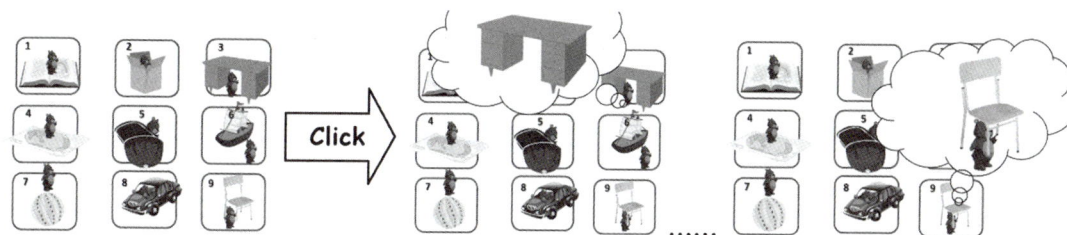

S1：(Is it under the desk?)

T：(T clicks the third picture and the PPT will show the answer.) Look at the picture. Is it under the desk?

Ss：(No, it isn't.)

S：. . .

S2：(Is it under the chair?)

T：(T clicks the last picture and the PPT will show the answer.) Let's see! Is it under the chair?

Ss：(Yes, it is.)

【设计说明】 通过猜测玩具熊的位置,引发学生好奇心,激活英语学习兴趣,同时复习核心句型。

Step 2　Pre-reading (8 mins)

Activity 1：Tidy up the schoolbag

Look at the pictures and help Zoom to tidy up his schoolbag. The teacher and students act as Zoom and Zip.

T：Great! We find the toy bear. It's Zoom's toy bear. Now it's eight o'clock. It's time to go to school. Zoom is tidying up his schoolbag. He can't find his book. (T acts as Zoom.) Where is my book?

S1：(Is it under the desk?)

T：Let me see! No, it isn't. (T clicks the picture and shows the answer.)

S2：(Is it on the chair?)

T：Yes, it is. Now we should put the book in . . .

S3：Put the book in the schoolbag.

Then students work in pairs and act as Zoom and Zip. They can help Zoom to tidy up his schoolbag. They can choose one-star task or two-star task to make up a new dialogue.

☆	☆☆
Zoom：Where is my book? Zip：Is it under the desk? Zoom：No，it isn't. Zip：Is it on the chair? Zoom：Yes，it is. It's on the chair.	Zoom：Where is my book? Zip：Is it under the desk? Zoom：No，it isn't. Zip：Is it on the chair? Zoom：Yes，it is. It's on the chair. Zip：Put your book in the schoolbag. Zoom：OK！

【设计说明】 同伴合作对话,运用核心句型询问和猜测物品位置并做出回答。学生根据自己的水平选择星级任务,分层任务充分尊重学生的差异性,鼓励所有学生参与到课堂活动中。

Activity 2：Look and predict

Look at the picture and predict where Zip is.

T：Zoom and Zip are in the classroom. They are playing "hide and seek". Where is Zip? Can you guess?

Ss：...

T：Maybe you can pay attention to the footprints.

Ss：...

T：You have your own guessing. Next，let's read to check it.

【设计说明】 看图预测 Zip 的位置,学生运用句型合理猜测,初步构建文本的意义,训练预测看图的阅读技巧。

Step 3　While-reading (20 mins)

Activity 1：Skim, circle and number

Skim the text, circle the words about the items and then number the pictures.

T：Now，let's skim the text, circle the words about items，and then number the pictures. For example，in the first sentence "Is it on the boat"，you can circle the word "boat"，and then write the number "1" on the picture of the boat.

Ss：...

T：Let's check. No. 2 "Is it under the chair?" The key word is ...?

S1：(Chair.)

T：So which picture is No. 2?

S1：(No. 2 is the picture of the chair.)

...

Read and number Tips: 圈出有关物品的单词, 标序号。

1. Is it on the (boat)? ☐
2. Is it under the (chair)? ☐
3. Is it on the (map)? ☐
4. Is it in the (desk)? ☐
5. Is it on the (ball)? ☐
6. Is it in the (bag)? ☐

Where is Zip?

【设计说明】 通过快速阅读文本, 查找每个句子中关于"位置"的关键词如 boat, chair 等词, 同时找到单词所指的图片并标上序号, 进行图文配对, 培养学生理解层次的认知能力。学生能够精准地在以上位置寻找 Zip, 为下文判断 Zip 的位置做铺垫。

Activity 2: Read and underline

Read the text carefully, pay attention to the phrases with prepositions "in/on/under", and underline these phrases.

T: Now read again, and pay attention to the phrases with prepositions. For example, in this sentence "Is it on the boat", you can underline the phrase "on the boat".

Ss: ...

Activity 3: Read and tick or cross

Read the text, and tick or cross. When they show their answers, they should say, "Yes, it is." or "No, it isn't."

T: This time, you can read and tick or cross. For example, "Is it on the boat?"

S1: (No, it isn't.)

T: So we should cross.

T: Now it's your turn to read, tick or cross.

Ss: ...

【设计说明】 通过细读文本捕捉关键信息, 判断 Zip 的准确位置。

Activity 4：Imitate

A. Imitate.

While imitating the video，students must pay attention to the rising tone when they read the general questions.

B. Read in groups.

Read in groups，and the top students in the group can help the slow students.

【设计说明】 通过听音模仿,运用正确的语音语调朗读课文;小组合作朗读文本,相互帮助,培养合作学习的能力,达到资源的优化配置。

Step 4　Post-reading (7 mins)

Activity 1：Read about "Careless John"

Reading text

John：Let's go home.

Amy：OK！

John：My books, my pen, my cap . . . Oh, where is my ruler?

Sarah：Is it in your pencil box?

John：No, it isn't.

Sarah：Is it in your desk?

John：No, it isn't. Where is it? Where is it?

Amy：Look, it's under your schoolbag.

John：Oh, yes. Thank you very much.

A. Look and guess.

Look at the picture and try to guess："Where is John's ruler?"

T：It's time to go home. Amy，Sarah and John are tidying up the schoolbag. Look at the picture and guess："Where is John's ruler?"

Ss：Is it . . . ? (T writes down students' answers on the blackboard.)

B. Read and judge.

Read the dialogue and judge their answers.

T：Let's read the dialogue and judge. If the answer is wrong，you can answer："No, it isn't." If it is right，you can answer："Yes, it is."

C. Role-play.

Role-play the dialogue，and pay attention to the stress and the intonation.

【设计说明】 图片的直观呈现,能吸引学生的兴趣,激活学生参与活动的热情;通过看图猜测和细读文本检测他们的预测,使学生获得活动的成就感,培养学生推理层次的认知能力;通过角色扮演朗读文本,练习正确的语音语调;熟悉对话结构,为下文小组合作编对话做铺垫。

Activity 2：Make up a new dialogue

Work in groups of 3 and make up a new dialogue.

John：Let's go home.

Sarah：OK!

John：My . . . Oh，where is . . . ?

Amy：Is it in/on/under . . . ?

John：No，it isn't.

Amy：Is it in/on/under . . . ?

John：No，it isn't. Where is it? Where is it?

Sarah：Look，it's under your schoolbag.

John：Oh，yes. Thank you very much.

Sarah：Put your . . .

John：OK! Now let's go home!

【设计说明】 学生综合运用单元知识,在具体的情境中完成对话,巩固了所学词汇和句型,同时培养了合作学习的能力和语用层次的认知能力;通过编创关于粗心 John 的对话,学生能够注重自身的日常习惯,养成收拾整理物品的好习惯。

六、 作业布置

1. Read the text for three times.

2. Act out their new dialogues in groups.

【设计说明】 学生课后练习对话有助于巩固课上学习的词汇和句型,更好地掌握一般疑问句结尾的升调处理,改进自身的语音语调。同时,学生的合作学习能力也进一步得到了提升。

七、 板书设计

Unit 4 Where is my car?

Where is...?		Is it on the desk?
It's in/on/under...	Is it in/on/under...?	Is it in the desk?
	Yes,it is.	Is it under the book?
	No,it isn't.	Is it on the chair?
		Is it under the pencil box?
		...

【设计说明】　板书呈现了本节课的重点词汇和句型,有利于学生了解和掌握单元重点内容。右边部分为学生回答的内容,体现了课堂的动态生成过程。

八、 教学反思

本节课属于小学低年级学段阅读启蒙课。教师以本课话题"寻找物品"为主线,一方面复习本单元的核心句型,另一方面引导学生初步感知和学习阅读策略,如看图预测,寻找关键信息的能力。本课的设计亮点有:

(一) 层层推进,提升学生思维品质

在本节课中,我非常关注对我们班学生思维品质的提升。我设计了图文配对活动,来培养学生的理解能力。此外,我多次设计了看图预测位置的活动,让学生通过思考推理来做出自己的猜测,提升推理分析能力。最后,我还给学生机会去创编对话,完成角色扮演,促进语用能力的提高。从理解到推理再到语用,层层推进,逐步培养学生的认知能力,提升学生的思维品质。

(二) 步步为营,培养学生阅读技能

小学低年级学段学生初次接触英语阅读,阅读能力较弱,教师设计了一系列活动,帮助学生理解文本,培养学生的阅读技能。首先,通过略读标序号的活动,学生圈出关于"位置"的单词,并在图片上标序号,进行图文配对;接着,教师设计了细读文本,划出关键信息的活动。学生在这一活动中关注 in/on/under 这些方位词获取关键信息。最后,学生能够根据前两步的铺垫,通过精读句子正确地判断。

(三) 合作学习,提高学生课堂参与度

在同伴合作活动的教学设计中采用分层任务设计的方式,鼓励每个学生参与到课堂活动中,使每个学生都有表现自我的机会;在文本朗读环节采用小组合作的方式模仿朗读文本,帮助后进生运用正确的语音语调朗读文本,引导每个学生都能积极参与学习活动。

(教学设计者:乐清南华寄宿学校　余琼梅)

主要参考文献

1. 方贤忠. 如何说课[M]. 上海：华东师范大学出版社,2008.

2. 刘显国. 说课艺术[M]. 北京：中国林业出版社，2000.

3. 罗晓杰. 多媒体辅助英语"说课"研究[J]. 外语电化教学,2003(6)：50-52.

4. 罗晓杰. 说课及其策略[J]. 教育科学研究,2005(2)：40-43.

5. 罗晓杰. 试论英语说课讲稿的撰写[J]. 课程·教材·教法,2002(4)：35-38.

6. 罗晓杰. 英语教学与教研[M]. 哈尔滨：黑龙江人民出版社,2003.

7. 罗晓杰,牟金江,项纸陆. 中学英语读写课教学设计与说课[M]. 长春：吉林文化音像出版社,2010.

8. 罗晓杰,牟金江. 如何说英语课——方法与艺术[M]. 上海：华东师范大学出版社,2012.

9. 罗晓杰,牟金江. 英语课堂提问策略研究[J]. 基础教育外语教学研究,2002(05).

10. 罗晓杰,叶志雄. 说课及其评价指标体系研究[J]. 黑龙江高教研究,2004(06).

11. 牟金江,罗晓杰. 布置与批改英语课外作业的有效策略[J]. 中小学英语教学与研究,2006(9)：16-19.

12. 罗晓杰,牟金江,项纸陆. 英语学科知识与教学能力(初中版)[M]. 上海：华东师范大学出版社,2013.

13. 牟金江,罗晓杰,项纸陆. 高中英语"三段七步"读写整合教学法[M]. 福州：福建教育出版社,2015.

14. 周玲,罗晓杰,项纸陆. 英语教师说课技能存在的问题与对策[J]. 基础教育外语教学研究,2011(3)：34-36.